"This book's highly readable chapters on speech and language development and language stimulation will be very helpful to parents. The chapter that assists parents in determining when professional services are needed and provides a process of evaluating the quality of those services is particularly strong."

—Sue T. Hale, MCD, CCC-SLP, director of clinical education and assistant professor in the Department of Hearing and Speech Sciences at the Vanderbilt Bill Wilkerson Center and former vice president for quality of services in speech language pathology of the American Speech-Language-Hearing Association

"I found the book to be a great resource. Every new parent should have a copy. I found the information to be accurate yet easily understandable to non-professionals. Its a great source of information for parents and parents-to-be."

—Nancy Patterson, president of the New Jersey Speech Language Hearing Association and a school-based speech-language specialist since 1972

"If your child has an articulation problem, Dougherty's book is a treasure. Her explanations are clear, her advice is sensible and down-to-earth, and the exercises she recommends arc clever and engaging. Most of all, she details developmental timelines that will enable parents to recognize and address problems properly, including advice on when and how to seek professional help. Her book is elegantly sensible, informative, and filled with reassuring common-sense strategies."

—Mary Joyce Perskie, vice president of the Bacharach Institute for Rehabilitation in Pomona, NJ

"Dougherty has written a wonderful book, which provides readers with insight into normal speech and language development and alerts them to warning signs of common communication disorders. This book will prove a worthwhile resource to any professional working with the pediatric population."

—*Patricia Maletto, MA, CCC-SLP, speech and language pathologist and certified member of the American Speech and Hearing Association*

"Dougherty's book is a gem. Preschool teachers nationwide need this book at ready reach. Families need a concise, friendly, easy-to-read, interesting place to learn about children with speech needs. The book gives parents straightforward answers to difficult questions while it offers practical help that enables parents to be involved teaching the children they love. This is a front-table book."

—*Judy Lyden, preschool teacher, director of the Garden School, and childcare Columnist for the Scripps Howard News Wire Reporter National Media Service*

"There are many books on the market that cover speech and language development, but Dougherty's approach is easy-to-read, down-to-earth, and reflective of her many years of experience working with children as a speech and language pathologist. She presents a natural approach to speech and language development that every parent can clearly understand. 'How to Find Professional Help' in chapter eight conveys precious information to busy parents who need to know how to help their child speak correctly."

—*Ellen M. Wright, Ed.D., educational specialist in early childhood*

"*Teach Me How To Say It Right* is a unique publication in the field of speech/language pathology. It's filled with current information and easy to use exercises that parents will find extremely helpful when working with their child. Dougherty has really filled a void with her abundance of knowledge and insight into the world of parenting a child with a communication disorder."

—*Kimberly King, speech/language pathologist in private practice focusing on preschool- through school-aged child*

"Every parent will want to reserve a spot on the bookshelf for this new classic. With its simple explanations and down-to-earth suggestions, parents will turn to this easy-to-read book time and time again with their questions on speech problems. Dougherty skillfully combines her training with years of on-the-job experience to give parents the answers. Not only a comprehensive reference guide on articulation disorders in children, this is a resourceful book that equips parents with knowledge, a developmental framework, and ultimately the confidence to understand their child's speech development. *Teach Me How to Say It Right* will get parents and their children off to the right start."

> —*Athena Coste, school psychologist for the Ocean City School District in Ocean City, NJ*

"For most parents, few events are more memorable than baby's first words. And, though they may hope their children master the language of their culture, many parents are concerned about their role in that acquisition. *Teach Me How To Say It Right* is a well-written, easy-to-read guidebook by which all parents may navigate the journey of their child's speech and language development. A gifted clinician, Dougherty has been able to distill the wisdom gained from more than two decades of personal research and experience into simple, down-to-earth, yet highly effective, activities. Applicable to both classroom and living room, this book provides the technical information and practical suggestions that empower parents and teachers to successfully promote speech and language development."

> —*Suzanne E. Tarasevich, Ph.D., director of special services for Ocean City Public Schools in Ocean City, NJ*

"Dougherty's book is an excellent guide to speech problems. Use these recommendations to guide your child and yourself through this learning process. I would highly recommend this book to any parent who wants to help their child speak clearly."

> —*Mary Beth Salmonsen, parent of a preschool child with a speech problem.*

Teach Me How to Say It **Right**

HELPING YOUR CHILD WITH ARTICULATION PROBLEMS

DOROTHY P. DOUGHERTY, MA, CCC-SLP

New Harbinger Publications, Inc.

Distributed in Canada by Raincoast Books

Copyright © 2005 by Dorothy P. Dougherty
New Harbinger Publications, Inc.
5674 Shattuck Avenue
Oakland, CA 94609

Cover design by Amy Shoup; Illustrations by Susan Schafer-Walker;
Edited by Kayla Sussell; Acquired by Tesilya Hanauer;
Text design by Tracy Marie Carlson

Library of Congress Cataloging-in-Publication Data

Dougherty, Dorothy P.
  Teach me how to say it right : helping your child with articulation problems / Dorothy P. Dougherty.
     p. cm.
  Includes bibliographical references.
  ISBN 1-57224-403-8
  1. Articulation disorders in children—Popular works. I. Title.
  RJ496.S7D68 2005
  618.92'855—dc22

                                   2005010579

New Harbinger Publications' Web site address:
www.newharbinger.com

08   07   06
10   9   8   7   6   5   4   3   2

I dedicate this book to my husband, Kevin, whose love and encouragement have guided me through my life.

Contents

Acknowledgments

I wish to thank my family and friends, especially my husband, Kevin, my mother, Dorothy Paglione-Rapp, and my sons, Nick and Tom, for their continuous love and support. Many thanks to my wonderful editors at New Harbinger: Tesilya Hanauer for believing in this project and Kayla Sussell for her invaluable writing expertise and kindness. I send my best wishes to all of the wonderful children I had the pleasure of helping as they learned to talk, and especially to Joseph Salmonsen and his big sister, Molly, who gave me the inspiration to write this book.

Foreword

Those of us blessed with children understand the sacred duty of helping our children to grow. Every day we must teach our children to care for themselves and others, to know right from wrong, and how to communicate with the world. As a person who lost her hearing when a young toddler, I remember the many things my mother did to guide and help me reach my highest potential. Parents are, most of all, the biggest and best role models for their children, and the only full-time teachers (twenty-four hours a day).

Many parents don't realize the important role they play in helping their child learn to talk. From my own experiences, I know that being able to communicate effectively with others leads to wonderful opportunities and helps a person to develop a sense of confidence. This book is about being involved in your child's learning from the moment of birth.

My family was always very involved in my education and, as a result, I have been able to pursue my dreams. *Teach Me How to Say It Right* will show you how to provide the most stimulating environment possible for your child to learn and grow. Dorothy Dougherty explains how important it is for every child to develop an early enjoyment of spoken and written language, especially those who may be having a difficult time learning to talk.

The numerous exercises you will find throughout the book will show you how to enhance your child's vocabulary and early literacy skills, and will encourage your child's ability to say sounds clearly and correctly. *Teach Me How to Say It Right* is written for all those who are parents of children from birth to age eight. It is never too early, or too late, to help your child to learn to speak.

My two young sons are the main priority in my busy life. Spending quality time with them is very important to me. Dorothy Dougherty explains easy and practical ways to turn the most routine activities into learning experiences that are fun to do. I remember my own mother helping me learn how to say words on our weekly trip to the supermarket. As we filled our cart, she encouraged me to speak the names of the various foods aloud.

The information provided in this book is practical but comprehensive. It is presented in an interesting and nontechnical manner. While you read, you will become familiar with how children learn to communicate. This information may help you to relax and pay close attention to your child's daily communication skills as they are developing. As you look forward to each developmental stage, your new knowledge will motivate you to listen closely and respond appropriately. The benefits your child will receive from this will last a lifetime.

Teach Me How to Say It Right also gives parents the information they need to take a good look at their child's speech, language, and hearing abilities and determine whether their child is developing as he or she should. If you want your child to lead a normal life, it is critical to make the right decision and begin interventions as soon as possible. Taking a "wait and see" attitude or, as in the case of a hearing-impaired child, deciding to wait for better technology, rather then giving your child the tools he or she needs now, may not be the best decision. I have seen the success children experience when they are given help at a very early age, and it is very impressive.

If you decide that you need to seek professional advice or help, chapter 8 is both very informative and very helpful. In this chapter, Dorothy Dougherty guides you through the process of finding a professional who can help your child. She explains what to expect and how to prepare yourself and your child for your first visit.

The author has spent her life educating parents about the important role they play in their child's speech and language development. I was happy to write this foreword because I believe all parents should have this information. From my own experience, I know that if you are raised in an environment that is fun, loving, and nurturing, the benefits last a lifetime and give you the power to pursue anything you desire. Begin early and give your child the skills he or she needs to follow their dreams.

—Heather Whitestone-McCallum—Miss America 1995
The first American with a disability to win the title

Introduction

As a speech/language pathologist for more than twenty-five years, I feel that I have the most wonderful job in the world. When I am able to teach a kindergarten child how to say her name, or a first-grader how to play a game with his friends, I feel as if I have given them an indescribable gift.

As adults, we often take talking for granted. We open our mouths, words come out, and people respond. For a young child with a speech-sound disorder, however, talking is often difficult. If young children are unable to express their thoughts and feelings, they may have difficulty developing relationships with other people, as well as difficulties with self-esteem, both of which, in turn, may cause them to become isolated from their peers. Parents often become frustrated and upset when they see their child struggling with something that comes so naturally for many children.

Because the age at which children master speech sounds may vary by as much as two years, parents often make comments and ask questions like these: "Will he outgrow this problem?" "Why does my daughter talk like this? My niece is a year younger and we can understand her when she talks." "How can I help my child talk more clearly?"

The purpose of this book is to give you information about articulation problems, as well as the knowledge to create a rich learning environment so that your child may say speech sounds when he or she is developmentally ready. Although not hard to understand, this book is also a comprehensive presentation of up-to-date information about articulation disorders.

In chapters 1 to 3, you will find information about speech-sound disorders: what they are, what their causes are, and how most children learn to say speech sounds. In chapter 4, you will find information about other communication problems that often coexist with articulation problems.

Chapters 5 to 7 will give you the tools you need to enhance your child's speech-sound learning and language skills. In chapter 8, you will learn how to seek professional help if it is needed, and how to prepare yourself and your child for the first visit to a speech/language pathologist.

In each chapter, you will find exercises. These exercises contain questions about your child's skills for you to answer. If you keep a separate notebook handy to write down your answers to these questions, that will not only be helpful, it will also allow you to get the greatest benefit from the book. I am sure that you want your child to grow to his or her highest potential in each developmental stage. The activities you will find here are fun, easy to do, and most of them can be done as you go about your daily routines.

This book is not meant to take the place of a professional consultation. If you have any concerns about your child at any age in any area, it is always wise to seek professional help as soon as possible. You are ultimately responsible for helping your young children communicate with the world. Relax and have fun as you help them reach their highest potential.

1 Learning to Communicate: Speech

Think about how many times today you've used words to pass on information, express your feelings, or influence others. How and what we say is an important part of who we are. Learning to communicate is a gradual process, and young children continually build on the skills they've already mastered.

For some children, saying words clearly and correctly is easy. However, others need a lot of practice before they can say all of the sounds of their language correctly. To provide your child with the most stimulating learning environment possible, it's important to understand speech-sound disorders. With this knowledge, you will be able to find the best ways to help your child learn. Having a basic knowledge of these speech-sound disorders may enable you to be more comfortable when speaking to your pediatrician or speech/language pathologist.

Moreover, removing needless worries about your child's development, as well as getting help with realistic problems, can make you feel more relaxed and open to enjoying the fun of helping your young child reach his highest potential.

SPEECH-SOUND DISORDERS

Speech is the actual physical production of sounds. If your child's speech sounds are different from his peers who are the same age, gender, or ethnic group, or if he frequently avoids talking because he is hard to understand, he may have a speech-sound disorder. Speech-sound disorders are widespread among children. Approximately 10 to 15 percent of preschool children and 6 percent of school-age children (grades 1 through 12) have speech disorders (American Speech-Language Hearing Association [ASHA] 2000).

When we talk, we put sounds together to form syllables, words, phrases, and sentences. For our message to be easily understood by others, sounds must be pronounced correctly. A child with a speech problem may understand words and phrases and use them to talk. However, people may have a hard time understanding his message because he has difficulty with one or more of the following areas:

- *Articulation* refers to the ability to produce speech sounds that make up syllables, words, and sentences.

- *Phonological processes* means mastering the sound patterns of a language.

- *Fluency* means the flow or rhythm of a person's speech. Problems with fluency are often referred to as "stuttering."

- *Voice* refers to how the speech sounds. For example, is the voice too loud, too soft, too hoarse, too harsh, or just right for the person's age? The quality of a child's voice may interfere with normal everyday activities or make the child's speech difficult to understand.

Articulation

A child with an articulation disorder does not pronounce words clearly and precisely because he uses the wrong sounds when speaking, or because he omits sounds in words. Articulation disorders are the most prevalent communication disorder. It has been estimated that three out of five of all speech and language disorders are related to articulation problems (ASHA 2000).

Types of Articulation Errors

Generally, children with articulation difficulties make the following kinds of errors: omissions; substitutions; distortions; and lisping. These errors can occur with a troublesome sound that can appear in the beginning, middle, or end of a word. *Example:* In "sun," the /s/ sound is in the beginning of the word. In "kissing," the /s/ sound is in the middle of the word. In "mouse," the /s/ sound is at the end of the word.

OMISSIONS

If the speaker leaves out a *phoneme* (a meaningful sound) in a word and does not replace it with any other sound, that is called an *omission error.* Even though omissions can occur in the beginning, middle, or at the end of words, they often occur in blends. A *blend* is two consonants said together, such as /bl/, /tr/, /sk/, /sn/.

Nick is four years old and his speech is characterized by the following sound omissions: omissions in /r/ and /s/ blends, and omission of /s/ in the middle position of words. Error examples include the following: "stick" is pronounced "sick"; "train" is pronounced "tain"; "baseball" is pronounced "ba-ball."

Parent: Where is your baseball?"

Nick: I left the "ba-ball" in the yard. (I left the baseball in the yard.)

SUBSTITUTIONS

A *substitution error* occurs when the speaker substitutes one speech sound for another. Grant is six years old and his speech is characterized by the following sound substitutions: /r/ is pronounced /w/; /k/ is pronounced /t/; and /ch/ is pronounced /s/. Error examples include the following: "ran" is pronounced "wan"; "milk" is pronounced "milt"; "chicken" is pronounced "sicten."

Parent: Would you like some more milk?

Grant: Yes, tan I have sotolate milt? (Yes, can I have
             chocolate milk?)

DISTORTIONS

If the speaker produces a sound that is modified in some way and is not completely accurate, it is a *distortion error*. A distortion may vary only slightly or sound extremely different from the standard sound. Mark is eight years old and his speech is characterized by distortions of /r/ sounds in all positions of words. Some words that are difficult for him to say include these: car, mother, bird, girl, door, and star.

Parent: Who is at the door?

Mark: The girl (distorted) who lives next door (distorted).

LISPING

If the speaker has a lisp, he uses a specific substitution involving one or all of the following consonant sounds: /s/, /z/, /sh/, /ch/, or /j/. These sounds are called *sibilants*. The /s/ and /z/ are the most common speech errors, as even minor variations are easily heard in these sounds. Many times a child will substitute a /th/ sound for an /s/ or /z/ sound.

Drew is five years old. His speech is characterized by a lisp on the /s/ and /z/ sounds. He often says "thun" for "sun"; "mithing" for "missing"; and "houth" for "house."

Parent: Did you have fun at the beach today?

Drew: Yeth, but the "thun" made the "thand" really hot."
             (Yes, but the sun made the sand really hot.)

MOST FREQUENT ERRORS

Children have the most difficulty saying the /s/, /z/, /r/, /l/, /sh/, /ch/, /j/, /th/, /k/, /g/, /f/, and /v/ sounds (McDonald 1964). They make the most errors saying these sounds when they fall at the end of words, such as the /s/ sound at the end of "house." They make the least number of errors saying these sounds at the beginning of words, such as the /s/ at the beginning of the word "sun."

PHONOLOGICAL DISORDERS

Phonology refers to the sound structure of our language. This structure is a collection of meaningful sounds called phonemes, and a set of rules that determine how these phonemes are arranged to make words. For example, the English language has forty-two phonemes. When we talk, we follow the rules of our language and use these phonemes in a systematic way to say words.

Even though it would be very difficult for most adults to list the rules governing how these phonemes are arranged to make English words, we've learned to follow these rules without even thinking about them. For example, the rules of English tell us that we should never begin a word with /ing/, and sometimes, even though we may add an /s/ sound to the end of a word, we pronounce it as a /z/ sound. *Examples*: "moves," "bugs," and "tabs."

Learning the Rules

When most children have acquired a speaking vocabulary of about twenty-five words, they begin to use the phonological system of their language. Of course, young children don't learn all the phonemes or the complicated rules governing their use; instead, most use phonological processes. A *phonological process* is a strategy used by children between one and one-half years to four years of age to simplify their production of adult speech sounds (Hodson and Paden 1981).

For example, when speaking, a young child may omit the final sounds in words. He may say "co" for "coat," and "co" for "comb." However, this child can pronounce the /t/ and /m/ sounds, because he is able to say "to" for "top" and "mil" for "milk." Therefore, his speech errors are not due to his inability to pronounce sounds, but because he has not yet mastered the rules that govern using these sounds in many words.

Some phonological processes are typical of normal developing children and disappear by age three or four. However, sometimes these errors persist and a child's oversimplification of sounds can make his speech very hard to understand. The goal of speech therapy is not to improve the pronunciation of individual sounds, but rather to eliminate the phonological processes.

Typical Phonological Processes

Some of the phonological processes often seen in young children include the following. Usually, these are dropped by most children by approximately three to four years of age.

- **Substituting easy, early developing sounds for those that are acquired later.** For example, /p/, /t/, /b/, /d/, /k/, and /g/ may replace /f/, /v/, /s/, /z/, and /sh/ in a young child's speech. *Examples:* "fish" is pronounced "pish," and "sun" is pronounced "dun."

- **Assimilating consonants in words or producing an incorrect sound in a word.** That is, the sound is similar to or influenced by another sound in the same word. *Examples:* "doggie" is pronounced "doddie"; "chicken" is pronounced "chichen"; "duck" is pronounced "guck."

- **Fronting: Consonants usually produced in the back of the mouth, such as /k/ and /g/ are replaced by sounds pronounced in the front of the mouth.** *Examples:* /k/ is pronounced /t/; "come" is pronounced "tome"; /g/ is pronounced /d/; "gum" is pronounced "dum."

Doug is three years old. He often assimilates consonants in words and substitutes early developing sounds for later developing sounds.

Parent: Where are your shoes?

Doug: My does are in the chichen. (My shoes are in the kitchen.)

Atypical Phonological Processes

Sometimes, a child's speech will be characterized by phonological processes not typical of normally developing children. According to Roth and Baden (2001) these may include:

- **Backing: Replacing sounds made in the front of the mouth with sounds made in the back of the mouth.** *Examples:* /t/ is pronounced /k/; "toe" is pronounced "koe"; /z/ is pronounced /g/; "zipper" is pronounced "gipper."

- **Omitting the first sound in a word.** *Examples:* "mice" is pronounced "ice"; "light" is pronounced "ight"; "yellow" is pronounced "ellow."

- **Glottal replacement:** A glottal sound is sound made in the voice box. /h/ is a glottal sound. A child who uses glottal replacements will substitute a glottal stop for a consonant. *Examples:* "bottle" is pronounced "bo –hle"; "chicken" is pronounced "chi –hen."

Maria is five years old and her speech is characterized by the deletion of initial consonants and backing.

Parent: How many pieces of bread do you want?

Maria: I ant koo. (I want two.)

FLUENCY DISORDERS

Fluency disorders are often called stuttering. *Stuttering* is a speech disorder characterized by an interruption in the normal flow of speech. According to a fact sheet on stuttering by the National Institute on Deafness and Other Communication Disorders (NIDCD 1997) approximately three million Americans stutter. Parents are often confused because a child may begin to stutter in a severe manner suddenly (Yairi and Ambrose 1992). Most people who stutter begin before they are five years old, and almost no one begins to stutter after the age of twelve unless they suffer a serious head injury.

Types of Disfluencies

Disfluencies are interruptions in the normal flow of speech. Occasionally when speaking, we all repeat a word, phrase, or sound, and/or we insert the interjections "uh" and "eh." These types of interruptions in our speech are considered normal and usually do not warrant concern. Stuttering, on the other hand, is a complex disorder and is sometimes hard to characterize. Most experts agree, however, that when a person stutters, the normal flow of his speech is characterized by some of the following interruptions or disfluencies. One or many of these disfluencies may often occur in the speech of someone who stutters.

- **Repeating sounds:** A person who stutters may repeat sounds (*Example:* "t-t-t-Tom"; and/or syllables (*Example:* "base-base-baseball").

- **Prolonging sounds:** A person who stutters may stretch out a sound or a syllable (*Example:* b . . . bucket).

- **Pausing or hesitating:** A person who stutters may pause or hesitate between words. He may have periods of silence in which it appears as if he is trying to talk, but no sounds or words come out of his mouth.

- **Secondary related behaviors:** A person who stutters may tense the muscles in his lips, jaw, and/or neck. The listener may notice tremors, eye blinks, and/or head turns. These behaviors often vary from person to person.

Is Your Child Stuttering?

Between two and seven years of age, your child's speech and language skills grow rapidly. As he learns new words and new sentence structures, and, at the same time, develops coordination of the muscles used for talking, he'll experience many new demands on his communication skills. Most children between two and four years old will display disfluencies as part of their normal language-learning process (Gregory and Hill 1993). However, for some children, their disfluencies are the beginning stages of stuttering.

NORMAL DISFLUENCIES

In the initial stages, stuttering may be difficult to recognize, because most children who are beginning to stutter often sound a lot like their age peers much of the time. It is important to consult a speech/language pathologist if you have any concerns about a young child's disfluencies at any age.

Most typically developing children between two and four years old will display the following kinds of normal disfluencies (Gregory and Hill 1993):

- Hesitates when speaking, or silently pauses.

- Interjects sounds, syllables, or words when speaking. *Example:* "Will you come come with me?"

- Repeats whole words, phrases, or sentences while speaking. *Example:* "I . . . I . . . want to do it myself."

- Repeats a word and uses the vowel sound normally found in the word. *Example:* "ba-ba-baby" rather than "buh-buh-baby."

- Has nine or fewer disfluencies in every one hundred words he says.

EARLY SIGNS OF STUTTERING

In contrast, a child who is at risk for stuttering may exhibit these early signs of stuttering when he speaks:

■　Stretches out a sound, such as "b . . . aby," longer than one second.

■　Repeats parts of words, rather than whole words or phrases. *Example:* "I got a c . . . c . . . coat."

■　Repeats more than one syllable in a word. *Example:* "Amermericaca."

■　Substitutes an "uh" vowel for the vowel in the word. *Example:* Instead of saying "bay-bay-baby," he substitutes "buh, buh, buh, baby."

■　The pitch and loudness of the child's voice increases when he repeats or prolongs sounds and syllables.

■　The child exhibits an uncontrollable quivering of his lips or tongue when he repeats or prolongs sounds or syllables.

■　The child appears frightened when he tries to say a word that is giving him trouble.

■　The child appears to have breathing difficulties or speaks in spurts, as if he's struggling to keep his airflow and voice flowing.

■　The child has ten or more disfluencies in every one hundred words.

■　The child may use a broken rhythm during a repetition of a sound ("b, b, . . . bike").

How to Help

To ensure that your child continues to see talking as a positive and wonderful experience, Patricia King, director of Temple University's Speech/Language Hearing Center, says you should do the following:

Create a fluency-enhancing environment around your child. Take everything down a notch by using a slower rate, and a nice, calm onset of sounds. Reduce talking demands and avoid asking many "wh" questions, "What's this?"; "Where's that?"; "Who is this?" (King 2002, p. 16)

King says researchers have found that when you create a soothing environment around your child, you give him the confidence to try to speak, and this can have a wonderful effect on his fluency:

> Reducing facial signs of stress is also very important. Don't be afraid to gently acknowledge the "stuck" speech and reassure the child that it's okay. Saying the stuttered word and having the child repeat it will assure him that the word or sound is not dangerous and can be said fluently. (King 2002, p. 16)

EXERCISE 1: Speaking to a Young Child

During all stages of development, while talking or listening to a young child, you should be able to answer yes to the following questions:

1. Do you speak slowly?   Yes _____ No _____

    Using a slow, unhurried, and relaxed speaking pattern will help your child view talking as a leisurely activity that's easy to copy. Young children should not feel pressured to talk. Neither should they have to rush to keep up with the conversation.

2. Does your facial expression, eye contact, and tone of voice show your child that you're interested in what he has to say? Yes _____ No _____

    If your child rushes in eagerly wanting to tell you something, try to stop what you are doing and give him your undivided attention. Establish eye contact and sit or bend down so that you are at the same height. Show that you are interested in what he has to say by asking questions. If your child has a hard time getting the words out, use easily answered questions, such as those that require only a yes or no answer rather than long explanations. Show him by your facial expression that you are listening to *what* he is saying, rather than *how* he says his words.

3. Do you allow your child time to finish talking without interruptions?   Yes _____ No _____

    As preschool children learn to express their ideas and opinions, it's important that you wait patiently and allow your child extra time to finish his words and sentences. Avoid filling in words or ideas you think he is trying to say. Wait a few second before you comment on something he has just said, so that if he wants to continue his thoughts, he can begin again without feeling the need to rush.

4. Do you try not to make suggestions to your child about how he should speak?   Yes _____ No _____

    Suggesting that your child should talk in a different way or making statements like "Take your time" or "Think about what you say before you say it" actually may cause him to feel uncertainty or anxiety about talking. If he appears upset or frustrated by his disfluencies, try to reassure him with a special touch, a hug, or your caring words.

Without Rhyme or Reason

    It's not uncommon for your child's disfluencies to disappear for several days or even weeks, only to return again. Although normal disfluencies, as well as stuttering, can occur without rhyme or reason, be aware of the conditions in your home, school, and neighborhood that may affect your child's speech. When it appears to be difficult for him to speak fluently, decrease his need to talk by focusing on enjoyable nonverbal activities, such as playing sports, watching television, or going for a walk together. Ask questions that will elicit short simple responses. *Example:* "Did you have fun at the playground today?" rather than "Tell me what you did at the playground today."

    Take advantage of those days and weeks when your child is more fluent by increasing opportunities for him to talk by joining in activities that involve speech, rhymes, and songs. Stage puppet plays, play verbal pretend games, or visit or shop where he'll have many opportunities to talk.

Understanding Your Child's Speech

"I'm talking here. Why don't they answer me?" Aine, now a third-grader, explains how she felt when people didn't understand what she was trying to say. Children often feel frustrated when they must say their words over and over again and no one seems to understand. Often parents share their frustration, too.

Intelligibility of speech refers to how well your child's words are understood or comprehended by others. The factors that affect whether a child's speech is easy to understand or unintelligible (not capable of being understood) vary from child to child. Often parents will ask, "Why can't I understand my own child?"

Children's intelligibility will vary depending on the situation, what information they are trying to convey, and the listener. Sometimes, your child may not be speaking unintelligibly, but what is going on around him may make him easier or harder to understand. Some of these factors include:

■ **Your child's familiarity with the listener:** How familiar the child is with the person he is speaking to works both ways. If the listener is familiar with your child's speech, or if your child feels comfortable and confident talking to a particular person, it may make his speech easier to understand.

■ **Environmental clues:** What's happening in the natural environment can help you understand what your child is saying. For example, if your child tells you a story about the paper hearts he made in school for Valentine's Day, this would probably be easier to understand on February 13 rather then in July. Also, it may help if your child is able to show you or use gestures to help you understand.

■ **Your child's emotional status:** When your child is upset, anxious, angry, or excited, his speech may be harder to understand.

■ **Your ability to listen closely:** If there is a lot of noise or activity going on around your child when he is trying to talk, it may be difficult for you to focus on his words and hear his message.

EXERCISE 2: Intelligibility Quiz

Check the items that pertain to your child. If you check one or more of these problem areas, that may give you some insight into why your child's speech is hard to understand.

- ☐ Your child has many errors in his speech-sound productions. Generally, the more errors a child has, the poorer the intelligibility of his speech.

- ☐ Your child makes many different types of sound errors. For example, he may substitute and omit sounds in words.

- ☐ Your child has inconsistent errors. For example, he pronounces /sh/ in the beginning of a word, such as "shoe," but he omits the /sh/ sound in the beginning of "shower."

- ☐ Your child makes errors in vowel sounds. A *vowel* is a sound in spoken language that is made by opening the vocal tract. English vowels include: /a/, /e/, /i/, /o/, /u/, and sometimes /y/.

- ☐ Your child speaks very fast, or very slow, or goes from fast to slow in one sentence.

- ☐ Your child simplifies words and communicates in short phrases and sentences.

- ☐ Your child's voice is too loud, too soft, or inappropriate for specific situations.

- ☐ Your child's voice quality is unusual. For example, his voice may sound as if all of the sounds come through his nose rather than his mouth. At times, the listener focuses more on the quality of his voice, rather than on the words he says.

- ☐ Your child's normal flow of speech is often disrupted by hesitations or sound and word repetitions.

2 How Do Speech Sounds Develop?

Have you ever found "sells on the beas" (shells on the beach) or made "totowate tip totties" (chocolate chip cookies) for a special holiday with your two-year-old child? Often, your child's pronunciation of sounds is endearing and not a cause for concern. That's because even though saying words clearly is easy for some youngsters, others need a lot of practice before they can say all of the sounds of their language correctly.

According to the American Speech-Language-Hearing Association (ASHA 2000), by the time a child is three years old, family members and caregivers should be able to understand his speech; at four years old, people with whom he doesn't associate regularly should be able to understand his speech; and by five years old, your child's speech should be understood by most listeners in all situations. However, many children do not learn to say all speech sounds at once; instead they develop their ability to say sounds in a predictable sequence. For example, children usually learn to say the /b/ sound, as in "ball," before they can say the /r/ sound, as in "run." This sequence of sound development begins at birth and may continue through the eighth year of life.

Since the normal development of speech sounds can vary by as much as two years, parents often feel more at ease when their child develops on the fast side of normal, rather than the slow side. Parents of children who cannot say all sounds correctly often ask, "Is this a stage?" "When should I seek professional help?" "Why does my niece talk clearer than my son, and she is almost a year younger?" In my experience as a speech/language pathologist, I've seen that not having the answers to these questions sometimes puts pressure on a family, and can even foster tension between family members.

Because both expecting too much and expecting too little may be harmful, it's important to know if your child's ability to say speech sounds is developing and progressing at an acceptable rate. This chapter outlines guidelines for the order in which children usually develop speech sounds and describes the sounds that children are expected to be able to say at certain ages.

Note that these are simply guidelines, and it is always wise to seek professional help if you have any questions about your child's development in any area. The information in this chapter may give you the knowledge you need to determine whether your child is developing speech sounds as he should. Also, if your child has had a speech evaluation and the speech/language pathologist has determined that he doesn't need speech therapy at this time, this chapter may put you more at ease with that decision.

To understand why a child may not pronounce sounds correctly, it's important to understand how sounds are made and how children practice saying them before they can combine them into meaningful words. Learning the stages your child will go through before he can combine sounds into words is very interesting. While you look forward to each developmental stage, your knowledge and interest in how his speech develops will motivate you to listen closely and respond to your child's verbalizations. The benefits your child receives from being heard and answered will last a lifetime.

HOW DO WE TALK?

Speech is made up of the sounds we make when we communicate a message by using words. It is an extraordinary and unique motor skill.

We produce six to nine syllables a second, which is faster and involves more motor fibers than any other human mechanical activity (Kent 2000). For a baby to learn to talk, certain physical and sensory conditions must exist.

Physically, the child must have lungs for air power, vocal cords that vibrate and make sounds, a tongue, lips, and a palate to shape the air into meaningful sounds, and a functioning brain to receive and send messages. The child must be able to hear the words spoken to him and be able to see and focus to learn the names of objects and actions. He must be aware of how things feel, especially around his mouth, to learn how to position his lips and tongue to make the different sounds. He must be able to organize and make sense out of what he sees, hears, touches, and tastes.

Speech begins when air is exhaled from the lungs (respiration). This air passes from the lungs to the larynx (phonation). Next, the sounds produced in the larynx are shaped into specific sounds by moving the tongue, lips, teeth, and palate (articulation). All of this happens while we speak under the brain's direction.

Respiration

Respiration is breathing. Our lungs are the energy source for breathing. Breathing for speech is basically the same process we use when we breathe to stay alive. When we inhale, air flows into our lungs. When we exhale, air flows outward and upward from our lungs. This airflow gives us the energy to produce speech sounds.

Phonation

Phonation is what happens in our larynx and vocal cords that enables us to produce audible sounds. The human larynx is located at the top of the windpipe. Shaped like a box, it has two small muscular folds on each side. These are our *vocal cords*, also called *vocal folds*. When air passes between these two folds, it vibrates, producing sounds that are the basis of speech. The position of the folds changes, which affects the way they vibrate and results in different voice qualities, such as pitch levels (how high or low the voice sounds) and tones (specific qualities of the voice, such as a childish treble or a cracked aged voice).

A *voiced sound* is produced when the vocal folds vibrate. This vibration is caused by an overpressure of air in the lungs. This produces an audible buzz. Place two fingers on the middle of your throat and say /z/. You will feel the vibration in your vocal folds and hear a buzz or voiced sound. If the vocal folds don't vibrate during sound production, the sound that is produced is voiceless—it has no buzz. Now, place two fingers on the middle of your throat and say /s/. You will not feel your vocal folds moving or vibrating.

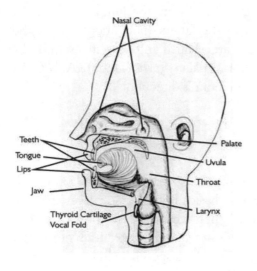

Articulation

Articulation refers to the ability to say individual speech sounds. To say sounds clearly, we must control and move our articulators. Our *articulators* include our lips, teeth, tongue, jaw, and various areas of the roof of our mouth (front, hard, and soft palate). If you raise your tongue to the top of your mouth, you can slide it over the roof of your mouth to feel the front, hard, and soft palates. (You can feel the difference between the hard and soft palates by moving your tongue as far back over the roof of your mouth as you can.)

The position and movement of these articulators determine the actual sounds that come from the mouth. Because we don't usually communicate using individual sounds but, instead, we rapidly combine the forty-three distinct speech sounds of English to form words, these articulators must be able to change positions very rapidly and precisely. To articulate properly, you must also be able to:

1. Move and place your articulators in the proper relation to each other, as described below:

    ■   Lips. We use our lips frequently when we speak. We press them together to make the /p/, /b/, or /m/ sounds. We position our teeth on our lower lip to produce the /f/ and /v/ sounds. We round our lips to make the vowel sound /u/.

    ■   Tongue. Our tongues can move to many different places and change into different shapes. If you place the tip of your tongue behind your upper teeth, you can make the /t/, /d/, /l/, and /n/ sounds. When you put your tongue between your teeth, you can make the /th/ sound.

    ■   Soft palate. During speech, the soft palate is raised. This prevents air from escaping through the nose. When we touch the lower side of the soft palate with the tongue, we can make the /k/ and /g/ sounds.

2. Control the stream of air coming from your lungs.

    ■   /p/, /b/, /t/, /d/, /k, /g/: When we make these sounds, we stop the air and then release it with a little explosion. These sounds are called *plosives*.

    ■   /s/, /z/, /f/, /v/, /sh/, /zh/, /th/: When we make these sounds, air passes through our partially closed articulators. These sounds are called *fricatives*.

3. We must know whether to make a voiced sound (buzz) or voiceless sound (no buzz).

    ■   All of the vowel sounds in English are voiced: (/a/, /e/, /i/, /o/, /u/).

    ■   All of these sounds are voiceless: /p/, /t/, /k/, /j/, /f/, /s/, /sh/, /ch/, /th/. (The last one is the /th/ sound at the beginning of "thumb" and at the end of the word "bath.")

    ■   All of these sounds are voiced: /b/, /d/, /g/, /z/, /j/, /m/, /n/, /ng/, /l/, /r/, /v/, /w/, /y/, and /th/. (The last one is the /th/ sound in the beginning of "this.")

PRACTICING SPEECH SOUNDS BEFORE THE FIRST WORD

Before most children can say real words, they communicate with a wide range of sounds, gestures, and facial expressions. As your child grows, he will develop control over the physical parts that enable him to speak, and he will continuously expand and change the sounds that he can make. These sounds, or vocalizations, develop through the following series of predictable steps at approximately the ages indicated. Knowing what to expect and how to respond to your baby will enhance his ability to make speech sounds.

Birth to Two Months: Discover Your Child's Style

Your child was born with his own special way of relating and discovering the world. Beginning shortly after birth, babies learn to control their mouths and airflow by coughing, burping, and crying. However, even in their first months of life, babies show a lot of variation in their interests, attention spans, and how they adapt to different situations and their surroundings.

Focus on your baby's individual style of communicating with you, and discover the differences between a cry of hunger and a cry of discomfort, or a genuine smile and a grimace from an upset stomach. Watch, listen, and respond to your baby's cues, and quickly give him the smile, food, or diaper change he's requested. It's important to tune into your baby's individuality and earliest forms of communication and respond appropriately so that he will learn his needs are important and his behaviors and verbalizations have an effect on others.

Two to Four Months: Cooing

Around two to four months of age, babies begin to coo, squeal, and gurgle. These sounds are regular and repetitive, and they sound as if the baby is making vowel sounds ("ah—ah," "ooh–ooh"). Many babies like making these dovelike coos when they are content. The coos vary in pitch—some sound high and some sound low. Most experts agree that in or around the sixth to seventh week of life, children are aware of the sounds they make and appear to enjoy making them.

Two to Seven Months: Vocal Play

Around two to seven months, babies like to entertain themselves by producing new sounds and repeating them. Vocal play occurs when babies begin using their voices to interact with their parents. The sounds they make continue to contain many vowels, such as "ee" and "aa." Because their throat muscles are not yet fully developed, these sounds are the easiest ones for them to make. As your child learns to explore his mouth with his tongue, several different types of sounds will emerge, and he will soon love to squeal, yell, and laugh out loud. Sometimes, he may even sound as if he is growling.

At around six months of age, babies begin to make sounds with their mouths partially closed. These sounds are called consonants. The first consonants that most babies add to their cooing are /k/, /p/, /m/, and /b/. For babies, these are the easiest consonant sounds to produce. At this point, most of the sounds your baby will make will be single syllables, such as "baaa," or "maaa."

Six Months of Age: Babbling

Beginning around six months of age, babies become better at controlling their vocal apparatus to repeat sounds and to babble. When your baby enjoys randomly putting vowels and consonant sounds together and repeating them over and over again, he is babbling. His favorites may include "baba," "kaka," and "mama." Your infant is learning that new sounds can be made by changing the shape of his mouth.

Nine to Twelve Months: Jargoning

Beginning somewhere around the ninth to twelfth month, your baby's babbling will include many more sounds. These sounds are strung together into phrases and sentencelike series called *jargoning*. The baby "speaks" with tones and inflections and sometimes sounds as if he is speaking another language. Sometimes you can hear a real word among the jargon.

First Words

At around twelve months of age, most children can move their mouths, tongues, lips, and hard and soft palates in a meaningful way to say real-sounding words. A child's first word is usually the name of something or someone that he has heard often, and he understands its meaning. This first word is followed by more and more words. Sometimes the first or last consonant or syllable will not be pronounced clearly. It's helpful that most children continue to use gestures to help complete their thoughts.

EXERCISE 3: Playing with Sounds

You can expand your child's ability to vocalize by encouraging an increase in the frequency, variety, or quality of the vocalizations that he produces (Roth and Baden 2001). Experiment with the activities below:

1. When speaking to your baby, provide face-to-face contact.

2. Respond to his verbalizations, mouth movements, and hand gestures by imitating him. When he smiles and coos, smile and coo back. When he babbles ("baba"), repeat what he says.

3. Make new sounds for your child to imitate or add another sound to his babbling. *Example:* When he says, "baba," you say "babada."

4.   Interact with him by giving him a chance to respond to your verbalization before you begin talking again.

5.   When your baby is quiet, make one of his favorite sounds, and see if he imitates you.

6.   Play sound and gesture games, such as peekaboo.

7.   Sing, hum, and cuddle frequently.

8.   Introduce playful sounds. These are sounds that babies enjoy listening to and may try to imitate. *Examples:* motors ("vroom vroom"), chickens ("peep peep"), dog barking ("ruff ruff").

9.   Respond to your baby's attempts to communicate with you. If he points to an object and makes a sound, give it to him. Say the name of the object he requests.

10. Encourage him to imitate. Attach an unbreakable mirror with an accurate reflection to the side of his crib. Look in the mirror with him and make faces and sounds. *Examples:* Stick out your tongue and puff out your checks; click your tongue and smack your lips.

SAYING SOUNDS CORRECTLY

Even though most children can use meaningful speech by the time they are eighteen months old, many cannot say all the sounds of their language correctly. Since the ability to say specific speech sounds is acquired at different ages, your child may be developing speech sounds as expected for his age. The first sounds children usually make are mostly vowels. By approximately thirty months of age most children have learned to produce all the vowel sounds correctly. However, as you will see, for many children the ability to say consonant sounds develops more slowly.

Eighteen months: Generally, if your child is eighteen months old, you should be able to understand approximately 25 percent of what he says.

Two years old: Once your child is two years old, you should be able to understand approximately 50 to 75 percent of what he says.

Time to talk: A typical conversation with a two-year-old might go like this:

Parent: Look at the big boat.

Child: I tan wide it? (I can ride it?)

The Age of Sound Acquisition: Three Years and Older

Many studies have been done to determine the *age of sound acquisition*, which means the age at which a child is expected to have learned to say a particular sound. Researchers typically assess groups of children of different ages to learn the number of children who are able to say a particular sound correctly at each age level. From these assessments, an age of sound acquisition for a particular speech sound is determined. The age of sound acquisition is the age level at which 75 percent (sometimes 90 percent) of children in the study used a particular sound correctly when it appeared at the beginning, middle, and end of words (Smit et al. 1990). Research also has shown that the age of sound acquisition varies between boys and girls.

In many states, the age of sound acquisition is used to set standards that determine whether a child is eligible to receive speech therapy in the public school setting. For example, 90 percent of all children are able to make the /k/ sound by the age of three years and six months (Smit et al. 1990). If a child is five years old and continues to make errors on /k/ sounds, a speech/language pathologist may recommend that he receive speech therapy. However, if your child is three years old and cannot say the /k/ sound, this may not be considered a delay, because many children at this age are still learning to say the /k/ sound correctly.

Always keep in mind that every child is different and many factors, not just the correct pronunciation of speech sounds, will determine whether your child should begin speech therapy.

The statistics reported below show the level of sound acquisition for girls and boys who were three years of age and older (Smit et al. 1990). For each sound, you will find the age at which 90 percent of the children studied were able to make the specified sound at the beginning of words (for example, the /s/ sound at the beginning of "sun"); and the sound at the end of words (for example, the /n/ sound at the end of "sun"). Unless specified, the sound mastery refers to both boys and girls. For easy reference, you will find all the sounds a child of a particular age is expected to be able to say correctly listed for each age group.

THREE TO FOUR YEARS OF AGE

Experts agree that even though your three-year-old child may make sound errors, 75 to 100 percent of what he says should be understandable to family and caregivers. Generally, children are able to make the following sounds at three to four years of age (Smit et al. 1990).

/h/ *Example:* the initial sound in "hat"

/w/ *Examples:* the initial sound in "water" and the final sound in "row."

/p/ *Examples:* the initial sound in "pony" and the final sound in "hop."

/b/ *Examples:* the initial sound in "boy" and the final sound in "tub."

/n/ *Examples:* the initial sound in "nose" and the final sound in "run." Boys at three years. Girls at three years and six months.

/t/ *Examples:* the initial sound in "top" and the final sound in "coat." Boys at three years and six months. Girls at four years.

/d/ *Examples:* the initial sound in "doll" and the final sound in "red." Boys at three years and six months. Girls at three years.

/k/ *Examples:* the initial sound in "cow" and the final sound in "milk." Boys and girls at three years and six months.

/g/ *Examples:* the initial sound in "go" and the final sound in "log." Boys at four years. Girls at three years and six months.

/f/ *Example:* the initial sound in "fun." Boys and girls at three years and six months. Note that the final /f/ sound is acquired at a later age.

Time to talk: A typical conversation with a three-and-a-half-year-old boy might go like this:

Parent: Do you know where your shoes are?

Child: My tus are on the pors. I will det dem. (My shoes are on the porch. I will get them.)

FOUR TO FIVE YEARS OF AGE

Children who are between four and five years of age should be able to make the following sounds correctly: /m/, /h/, /w/, /p/, /b/, /n/, /t/, /d/, /k/, /g/, /f/. In addition, they should be able to make the /th/ (voiced) sound. *Example:* the initial sound in "this" and "them."

Girls at four years and six months. Boys at seven years.

Time to talk: A typical conversation with a four-and-a-half-year-old boy might go like this:

Parent: Do you want a cookie or a cracker?

Child: Can I has a cookie pease? (Can I have a cookie please?)

FIVE TO SIX YEARS OF AGE

Children who are between the ages of five and six years should be able to make the following sounds correctly: /m/, /h/, /w/, /p/, /b/, /n/, /t/, /d/, /k/, /g/, /f/, and /th/ (voiced). In addition, they should be able to make the following sounds:

/f/ *Example:* the final sound in "laugh." Girls and boys at five years and six months.

/v/ *Examples:* the initial sound in "visit" and the final sound in "love." Girls and boys at five years and six months.

/l/ in the final position of words; *Example:* the final sound in "ball." Girls at five years. Boys at six years.

/l/ in the initial positions of words; *Example:* the initial sound in "love." Girls at six years. Boys at seven years.

Time to talk: A typical conversation with a five-and-a-half-year-old girl might go like this:

Parent: Do you want to go to the park or the beach today?

Child: Wet's go to the beas today. (Let's go to the beach today.)

SIX YEARS AND OLDER

Children who are six years and older should be able to make the following sounds correctly: /m/, /h/, /w/, /p/, /b/, /n/, /t/, /d/, /k/, /g/, /f/, /th/ (voiced), /f/, /v/, and /l/. In addition, they should be able to make the following sounds:

/ng/ *Examples:* the final sound in "ring" and "bring." Boys and girls at seven to nine years of age.

/th/ (unvoiced; the sound we make when we do not use our voices). *Examples:* the initial sound in "thumb" and the final sound in "bath." Boys at eight years. Girls at six years.

/s/ *Examples:* the initial sound in "sun" and the final sound in "house." Boys and girls at seven to nine years of age.

/z/ *Examples:* the initial sound in "zoo" and the final sound in "bugs." Boys and girls at seven to nine years of age.

/sh/ *Example:* the initial sound in "shoe" and the final sound in "push." Boys at seven years. Girls at six years.

/ch/ *Examples:* the initial sound in "chicken" and the final sound in "march." Boys at seven years. Girls at six years.

/j/ *Examples:* the initial sound in "jump" and the final sound in "large." Boys at seven years. Girls at six years.

/r/ *Example:* the initial sound in "run."

vocalic /r/ (The sounds that /r/ makes when it follows a vowel.) *Examples:* the medial sound in "charcoal" and the final sound in "door" and "mother." Boys and girls at eight years of age.

MASTERING BLENDS

When two or three consonants are placed together in a word, that is called a *blend*. Children often have difficulty with blends. For example, the /st/ in "stop" is a blend. Children often omit one sound in the blend, such as omitting the /l/ in the /pl/ blend at the beginning of "please" and saying "pease"; or they substitute a sound in a blend, such as saying a /w/ sound instead of an /r/ sound in the /dr/ blend at the beginning of the word "draw." The pronunciation of draw becomes "dwaw."

Most children acquire the following consonantal blends at the ages indicated below (Smit et al. 1990).

/sp/, /st/, /sk/, /sm/, /sn/, /sw/, /sl/, /skw/, /spl/, /spr/, /str/, /skr/

Boys and girls at seven to nine years.

/pl/, /bl/, /kl/, /gl/, /fl/

Girls at five years and six months. Boys at six years.

/pr/, /br/, /tr/, /dr/, /kr/, /gr/, /fr/

Boys and girls at eight years.

Time to talk: A typical conversation with a seven-year-old girl might go like this:

Parent: Did you make any new friends in school today?

Child: Yes, Mawy sat next to me in sool. She has a bwotha named Gawey too. (Yes, Mary sat next to me in school. She has a brother named Gary too.)

RED FLAGS

As you can see, some children are not able to make all of the speech sounds of their language clearly until they are close to their ninth birthday. If you have any concerns or questions about your child's speech development, it is always wise to seek professional help as soon as possible to determine whether he needs speech therapy. (See chapter 8, How to Find Professional Help.)

3 What Can Cause an Articulation Problem?

If a child rushes indoors with a scraped knee from playing outside, the first question a parent usually asks is "What happened?" That's because when we know the cause of a problem, that often helps us find the solution. Many times, however, learning what might be causing a child to have articulation problems is not as easy as learning the cause of the child's scraped knee. This, in turn, may cause parents to feel guilty, worried, and at a loss as to what to do. In this chapter you will find an outline of some of the known and unknown causes and characteristics of an articulation problem. This knowledge may empower you to become part of the solution, and to know what to expect as your child grows.

Researchers have concluded that articulation problems can be attributed to functional articulation problems, environmental factors, and/or organic problems. The factors that influence speech and language development are a child's physical and mental development, and her home environment. Cleft palate, hearing impairment, low cognitive functioning, and apraxia are some of the physical and mental impairments that may interfere with a child's speech development.

FUNCTIONAL ARTICULATION PROBLEMS

A *functional articulation problem* is the inability to produce all of the standard sounds of a language. There is, however, no known cause for these difficulties. In other words, children with functional articulation problems have good hearing perception and intellectual ability, and no signs of structural abnormalities or brain problems. It's common for parents to feel perplexed when told their child has a functional articulation problem, and that her difficulties may be due to immature development, rather than to a known cause. However, it's comforting to know that most children who have functional articulation problems can learn the correct production of speech sounds over time.

GIANNA: FUNCTIONAL ARTICULATION PROBLEMS

Gianna is a first-grader, age six years and two months, who has been diagnosed with a functional articulation problem. Her hearing is normal and there are no known structural or physical problems contributing to her speech difficulties. Her classmates and teachers have a difficult time understanding what she says. Even Gianna's mom and dad sometimes don't quite get what she tries to tell them, especially when she is excited or talking very quickly, which she often does. Midway through first grade, Gianna is struggling. She can't name all of the letters of the alphabet and has a hard time hearing the differences between the sounds the letters make.

When Gianna speaks, she substitutes /t/ for /k/ in all positions of words. *Examples:* "cookie" is pronounced "tootie," "coat" is pronounced "toat," and "park" is pronounced "part." She substitutes /s/ for /sh/ and /ch/ sounds in words. *Examples:* "shoe" is pronounced "sue," "chicken" is pronounced "sicten," and "march" is pronounced "mars." Gianna omits /s/ and /l/ in consonantal blends. *Examples:* "skate" is pronounced "tate," "basket" is pronounced "batet," and "please" is pronounced "pease." Gianna and her first-grade teacher might have the following conversation:

Teacher: What color marker would you like?

Gianna: I will tat the bu one pease. (I will take the blue one please.)

ENVIRONMENTAL FACTORS

Environmental factors are the external influences or activities that take place in your child's world. According to Rima Shore (1996), the impact of environmental factors on a young child's brain development is both dramatic and specific. Environmental factors not only influence the general direction of development, they also affect how the human brain becomes "wired." It is now understood that what a child sees, hears, touches, and feels during the first years of life strengthens and shapes brain connections that will work together to foster learning throughout her life.

The amount and kind of speech and language stimulation and the presence of certain environmental conditions in your child's home will play an important role in her development of articulation skills. A home environment that provides lots of stimulation and interaction between parent and child not only enhances your young child's speech and language skills, it also makes the time you spend together fun and rewarding.

Family History

It is estimated that between 28 and 60 percent of children with a speech and language deficit have a sibling and/or parent who is also affected (Fox, Dodd, and Howard 2002). Early research found that firstborn children and only children have significantly better articulation skills than children with older siblings or children who are twins (Davis 1937).

The age span between siblings was also found to affect articulation. Children who were closer in age to their siblings had more difficulties. Many speculate that this is so because, in most cases, the amount of time a parent can spend with a child decreases with each child added to a family. Studies also found that girls often demonstrate slightly better articulation skills than boys, and that boys are also more frequently identified as having articulation problems than girls (Perkins 1977).

Good Models

Children imitate the patterns of articulation that they hear spoken around them. To develop normal patterns of speech, early research concluded that most children must hear normal patterns and have a need and desire to talk (Winitz 1969). A child may develop poor articulation skills if she is surrounded by people who do not say sounds precisely or accurately. Often, poor models can be busy parents, an older sibling with speech problems, or a caregiver or family member with poor speech with whom the child spends large amounts of time.

The Value of Lots of Stimulation

If a child doesn't receive a lot of verbal stimulation, or people in her environment don't acknowledge her or respond when she talks, in later situations she may choose not to speak. Children learn to say speech sounds correctly by listening to others talking directly to them and by practicing talking themselves. They must enjoy hearing speech and responding with words, and they must be reacted to constructively by others in their environment when they speak.

Some children have all of their needs and wants anticipated by parents, siblings, or others, without having to say any words, and they seldom have to practice using words to communicate. Sometimes, parents are able to interpret everything their child says, even if these same words are not recognizable by anyone outside the home. These parents may, in turn, become too tolerant of speech errors and not provide feedback or modeling of the correct pronunciations. The child doesn't need to try harder to get her message across or to speak more clearly in her home.

Emotional Reactions

Children may stop developing their articulation skills or regress to a more immature pattern as the result of an emotional reaction to a traumatic experience. This is not limited to, but may include, the birth of a sibling, hospitalization of a parent, or the death of an important person in their lives. This may also occur if a child undergoes a long hospitalization, illness, or injury.

EXERCISE 4: Take a Look at Your Child's Learning Environment

Are you providing the best environment possible for your child to learn and grow? You should be able to answer yes to the following questions.

1.   Are you a good model?

Modeling the correct way to speak will help your child learn the correct way to say speech sounds. Experts believe you should not use or encourage "baby talk." For example, it is much better to say, "You are hungry. Here is your bottle," rather than, "Me want babab, so hungy." Speak clearly, naturally, and, most important of all, correctly. Before your child speaks, she will listen to everything you say, and how you say it.

2.   Do you tune into your child and follow her lead?

As your child begins to communicate with you, focus on the words and objects that are central to her life, or on which she is focusing at the moment. For example, if she is pointing at a squirrel running up the tree, don't start talking about the dog across the street. Talk about the squirrel. For example, say, "See the squirrel? He has a bushy tail."

3.   Do melodies dance in your baby's brain?

All parents know instinctively that singing soothes a fussy baby. Psychologists believe that music enhances early brain development beginning in the earliest months of life. By exposing your child to music early in life, you may enhance her ability to understand information, hear the differences in sounds, and stimulate her ability to repeat words she hears. Many of your child's favorite toys will play music, and she will probably enjoy listening to the radio, stereo, or you, as you hum, whistle, or sing your favorite song.

4.   Are you part of the action?

When you play music for your child, sing, dance, and laugh along. Show your enjoyment and be part of the action. Although your baby is unique and may enjoy many different kinds of music, some experts think that newborns are best comforted by quiet, soothing music, including lullabies, love ballads, gentle blues, and folk songs. When your child sits on your lap, she may enjoy listening to you sing more upbeat songs, such as, "Row, Row, Row Your Boat," "The Itsy Bitsy Spider," and "Twinkle, Twinkle Little Star." Many of these songs have gestures that go with the lyrics. Show your child by your actions and words that you enjoy the time you spend together.

5.   Do you play with sounds?

Begin early, and give your child the experience of listening to many different sounds. Hearing the differences between sounds, or *auditory discrimination*, is a critical link to learning to say sounds correctly as well as learning to read. Comment on the sounds around you: Say, "Listen to the clock ticking," or ask, "Do you hear that airplane? It is loud." Talk about the sounds your child makes when she splashes in the tub, claps her hands, and stamps her feet. Bang pots with spoons, or drop blocks into different empty containers made of plastic, metal, or cardboard. Talk about the different sounds you hear when the block falls into each container.

6.   Do you make contact with your child's eyes?

Make eye contact before you begin to talk to your child. You might call her name or use another attention getter, such as "Hi" or "Look," to hold her attention longer. If your child looks away, repeat her name again to see if she is interested in continuing to play and talk with you. Use only one form of her name, as some experts believe that using more than one form (Tom, Tommy, Thomas) may be too confusing at an early age.

7.   Do you keep your talking concrete?

Speak clearly and slowly to your child about what is happening around her. If you speak at a slow but comfortable pace and enunci-ate clearly, it will be easier for her to learn how to say individual sounds and words. Also, use short phrases and sentences, so that she may grasp the rules of grammar more easily. However, don't abandon complex sentences completely. Research has shown that children who were exposed to longer sentences containing words like "because" and "which" learned to express these words earlier than children whose parents seldom used them (Huttenlocher et al. 2002).

8.   Do you repeat, repeat, repeat?

Play the same games and sing the same song over and over again. Your child will soon learn to anticipate your words and gestures. At around six months, your child may acquire a favorite book. Although reading the same book four times in one morning (at your child's request) may be tiring for you, the repetition will reinforce her learning. Reading the same words over and over will help her learn to make connections between the words she hears and the pictures she sees. A child must hear a word many times and understand its meaning before she will express it.

9.   Do you recognize and create learning opportunities?

Visiting a zoo, a hands-on museum, or an aquarium will provide your child with wonderful opportunities to learn about the world. However, these are not usually everyday excursions. Therefore, it's very important to learn to recognize the hundreds of opportunities that exist all around you every day to enhance your child's speech and language learning. Speech and language learning are not activities that you set time aside for each day; instead, they happen all day long as you simply, but attentively, talk with your child while you go about your daily life.

ORGANIC PROBLEMS

When the cause of an articulation problem is *organic*, it is the result of structural or brain problems. Some organic problems that often cause a child to have articulation problems include cleft palate, hearing impairment, apraxia, and problems with the muscles of the mouth used to make speech sounds.

Cleft Palate

When you look into a mirror and open your mouth, you can see that the *palate* (the roof of your mouth) extends from behind your front teeth all the way to the back of your mouth. If you run your tongue over the roof of your mouth, you can feel a seam down the middle. That is where your hard and soft palate grow together. When a child is born with a cleft palate, a birth defect that affects one in seven hundred babies, she has a split or cleft in the roof of her mouth that may prevent the soft palate from closing off the space between the nasal cavity and the mouth cavity. As a result, sounds that come directly through the mouth may be distorted or impossible for the child to make. Therefore, surgical repair of the palate is usually recommended before the age of one (before most children say their first word). A small percentage of children born with a cleft palate have a nasal tone to their speech, or "hypernasality," after surgery.

It is not unusual for a child born with a cleft palate to show a delay in the development of speech sounds during the nine- to twenty-four-months age range. Approximately 10 percent to well over 50 percent of children born with a cleft palate are prone to problems with language development, articulation, and nasality (Peterson-Falzone et al. 2001). These difficulties can be the result of many factors, including the following:

- scarring of the palate

- small gums as a result of a cleft repair

- poor movement of the soft palate

- fluctuating hearing level

Many such children do develop normal articulation with speech therapy; however, others may need additional surgeries.

MARIE: CLEFT PALATE

Marie is a five-year-old who was born with a cleft palate. A successful surgery to repair her cleft palate was performed before her second birthday. Marie's speech is characterized by an audible emission of air. Her voice is *hypernasal*, which means the air comes out of her nose when she speaks. The rhythm of Marie's speech appears to be physically demanding due to the nasal leakage of air, and she often seems to pause to breathe at the wrong time.

When Marie says a word with one of the following sounds, she may distort the sound, omit a sound, or substitute a different sound: /f/, /v/, /th/, /s/, /z/, /sh/, /k/, /g/, and /h/. Most of Marie's errors occur when these sounds occur at the end of the word. When saying a word that blends two consonants together, she may omit a sound. *Examples:* "please" is pronounced "pease," and "skate" is pronounced "sate."

HOW WE HEAR

To understand hearing loss, it's important to understand how we hear. Initially, sound waves are collected by the pinna. The *pinna* is the external ear or the part that can be seen. These sound waves travel through the ear canal to the eardrum and cause it to vibrate. Next, the vibrating eardrum causes the three tiny bones (the *ossicles*) in the

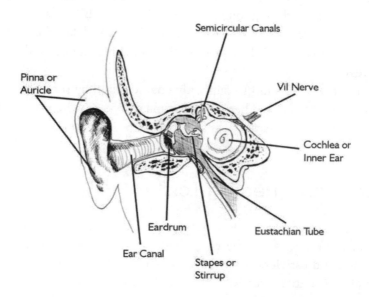

middle ear to vibrate. These sound vibrations go through an oval opening in the middle ear, called the "oval window," and travel to the cochlea in the inner ear. The *cochlea* is a bony snail-like structure filled with fluid and lined with hair cells.

The vibration of the ossicles causes a vibration in the oval window in the inner ear. When the oval window vibrates, the fluid in the cochlea moves. The fluid movements move the hair cells in the cochlea and this produces electrical impulses. These electrical signals travel to the brain along the auditory nerve, which connects the inner ear to the brain. When these signals reach the brain, we perceive sound.

HEARING LOSS

Hearing loss or hearing impairment happens when there is a problem with one or more parts of a child's ear (or ears) that prevents her from hearing sounds properly. When a child has a hearing loss, she faces the challenge of learning how to say sounds by watching what sounds look like on the face of the speaker, how they feel through vibrations, and what she hears through a distorted signal. It is estimated that, in the United States, one to six per one thousand newborns have congenital hearing loss at birth (Cunningham and Cox 2003). Early detection and intervention are critical because hearing loss will delay the development of speech and language skills, cognitive skills, and school progress.

Hearing loss is most commonly characterized by the parts of the ear that are affected. There are two major types of hearing impairments: conductive hearing loss and sensory hearing loss.

Conductive Hearing Loss

Conductive hearing loss occurs when there is a problem with a part of the outer or middle ear. These would include the ear canal, eardrum, and ossicles. A blockage or structural problem in the outer or middle ear interferes with the conduction of sound to the inner ear. This makes sound levels seem lower and may result in mild hearing loss that, in most cases, is not permanent. Medications usually clear up a conductive hearing loss and return a person's hearing to normalcy.

MIDDLE EAR INFECTION

Conductive hearing loss can result from excessive ear wax, a foreign object lodged in the ear, or water remaining in the outer ear after swimming or bathing. However, the most common cause of conductive hearing loss in children is an ear infection that affects the middle ear. The medical term for a middle ear infection is *otitis media*. Most ear infections occur between the ages of four months and three years, when children are listening to the sounds around them and learning to say words clearly. Approximately 80 percent of children up to four years of age experience otitis media (Zielhuis, Rach, and van den Broek 1989).

Why do children get ear infections? Because a young child's *Eustachian tube*, the passage that connects the middle ear to the throat, is shorter and straighter than that of an adult, germs travel there easily, and the middle ear fills with fluid. When the middle ear fills with fluid, the three tiny bones in the middle ear that carry the sound vibrations from the eardrum to the inner ear cannot transmit the sounds properly. This may result in a variable, temporary, and mild-to-moderate hearing loss (Gravel and Wallace 1998). That is why when children have an ear infection, the sounds they hear are not clear and precise.

If fluid from an ear infection remains in the ear untreated, your child will not get the full benefit of the language-learning experiences going on around her and she may develop speech or language problems that continue through her school years. Even a temporary mild hearing loss from an ear infection can slow a child's abilities to understand language and learn to say words clearly and correctly. Research suggests that a history of otitis media and mild hearing loss in the first year of life is associated with poorer academic abilities when a child reaches school age, particularly in reading skills and those skills that underlie reading (Gravel and Wallace 1995).

EXERCISE 5: How Will You Know If Your Child Has Otitis Media?

The symptoms, severity, and length of time that an ear infection persists vary considerably. Often, there are no signs of fever or pain. Because ear infections can affect children before they can speak or tell you something is wrong, weeks or months may pass before you realize that your child even has an ear infection. If you answer yes to any of the following questions, it's important to talk to your physician as soon as possible about your concerns:

1. Does your child shake her head often or tug or pull on her ears? This may result from a feeling of pressure or blockage in the ear. Yes _____ No _____

2. Do you see fluid draining out of your child's ear? This fluid may be thin and watery or thick and filled with mucus. Yes _____ No _____

3. Does your child appear to have decreased attention or seem to be suddenly withdrawn from others? Yes _____ No _____

4. Does your child appear to be dizzy? (You may notice falling or unusual clumsiness.)   Yes _____ No _____

5. Does your child appear unresponsive to surrounding sounds and actions?   Yes _____ No _____

6. Does your child appear to be irritable or experience sudden changes in her disposition? Yes _____ No _____

Generally, otitis media is not serious if it is diagnosed quickly and treated effectively. It's also important to compensate for your child's temporary hearing loss by talking louder than usual. When you read to her, point to the picture as you read the words. This will give her visual cues to make your message clearer and will help her to better understand the words she hears.

Sensory Hearing Loss

A sensory hearing loss occurs when there is a problem in the inner ear or in the nerves that send the sounds to the brain. This type of hearing loss is almost always permanent. The degree of hearing impairment may vary widely. If a child has a partial or mild hearing loss, the ear is able to pick up some sounds. However, if a child has a complete hearing loss, she cannot hear at all and is considered deaf. Hearing loss may affect one or both ears, and it may be worse in one ear than in the other.

Profoundly hearing-impaired or deaf children who have a loss measured at greater than 80 decibels (how loudness is measured) have great difficulty learning to speak even with intervention. Of course, how well a child learns to talk clearly is affected by many other factors, which may include the following (Quigley and Kretschmer 1982):

- The age of onset of the hearing loss. Children who are born with or who have a significant hearing loss before the age of three often have more severe articulation deficits than children whose losses occurred after the critical language-learning period, birth to three years.

- At what age the child was identified as having a hearing loss.

- When and how interventions are put into place for the child. The child's existing hearing is often maximized when she is diagnosed early in life and receives appropriate interventions, such as hearing aids, special therapies and programs, and/or *cochlear implants* (tiny electronic devices placed in the cochlea that turns sounds into electrical signals that directly stimulate the nerves for hearing).

- How the hearing loss affects their ability to hear specific sounds.

Causes of sensory hearing loss: Every day in the United States, approximately one to three infants per one thousand are born with a significant hearing loss. A child's sensory hearing loss may be the result of heredity, or genes passed down by her mother or father. According to the National Center on Birth Defects and Developmental Disabilities (2003), in about 30 percent of the babies who have a hearing loss, the loss is part of a syndrome that means these babies also have other problems. There are approximately four hundred syndromes that can cause hearing loss. Sometimes a serious infection, medicine, or severe injury to the head also can cause this type of hearing loss. If your child is frequently exposed to very loud music or very loud noises, this too can cause her hearing to become permanently damaged.

Detecting a hearing loss: Often, hearing problems are not obvious until a child fails to meet language-development milestones. Since the age at which children begin to say actual words varies widely, parents and pediatricians often don't suspect that something may be wrong with their child's hearing. The average age of detection of a significant hearing loss is approximately fourteen months (Task Force on Newborn and Infant Hearing 1999). As a result, many children are not diagnosed until they are two or three years old. Frequently, when hearing loss is not detected early, speech and language development, social and emotional growth, and academic achievement are delayed.

Modern technology now enables an audiologist to test the hearing of newborn infants and young children with great accuracy. *Audiologists* identify and assess disorders of the hearing and balance systems of children and adults. Audiologists select, fit, and dispense amplification systems such as hearing aids and related devices; program cochlear implants; and provide instruction, rehabilitation, and counseling services to enhance human communication.

Indicators for Hearing Loss

According to the American Academy of Otolaryngology-Head and Neck Surgery, if your newborn (birth to six months) does not move, cry, or react in any way to an unexpected loud noise, or if she doesn't turn her head in the direction of your voice when you speak, she may have a hearing loss (2003). Between six and twelve months, your child should be able to understand simple phrases and point to familiar persons or objects when asked. Between three months and two years, she should accurately turn in the direction of a soft voice on the first call and be alert to environmental sounds. If, at any age, she doesn't show consistent growth in her ability to understand and use new sounds and words, or if she suddenly stops babbling or talking, these may be signs that she has a hearing loss, and it would be wise to seek professional help.

SIGNS OF HEARING LOSS IN OLDER CHILDREN

These are some of the signs that may indicate that your child has a hearing loss:

- appears to strain to watch the face of the person who is speaking

- does not always pay attention when spoken to

- often gives the wrong answer to simple questions

- frequently asks the speaker to repeat words or sentences

- has frequent earaches, colds, running ears, upper respiratory infections, or allergies

- appears to function below her potential in school

- has behavior problems at home and in school

- is often withdrawn and moody

HEIDI: SENSORY HEARING LOSS

Heidi is eight years old and has a moderate sensory hearing loss that was detected shortly after her birth. She has been fitted with hearing aids in both ears. When speaking, Heidi omits final consonants: She says "hou" for "house" and "ba" for "bat." Heidi omits some consonants in blends: She says "sed" for "sled" and "pay" for "pray." She also omits some initial consonants: She says "ous" for "mouse" and "at" for "hat." Heidi substitutes a schwa vowel for other vowels, or adds this vowel to the end of words. The *schwa vowel* is a vowel produced in the middle part of the mouth. Typically, it appears in unstressed syllables. *Example:* The final vowel of "sofa" is a schwa vowel. Heidi also uses incorrect vowels in some words.

Heidi continues to demonstrate consistent progress in her ability to say speech sounds correctly. Her therapist attributes this to her involvement in early intervention services and the great support she receives from her family. She participates in speech and language therapy three times a week in her public school.

APRAXIA

Imagine that you know what you want to say, and you have good muscle strength and coordination, but your brain doesn't send the correct instructions to your tongue, lips, teeth, or palate to move in a specific way to make the correct speech sounds. This is called *speech apraxia.* It is a disorder of the nervous system that affects a child's ability to plan the motor movements needed to make sounds. Therefore, her ability to sequence and say sounds, syllables, and words is affected.

Some children with apraxia have developmental and communication problems as well as an articulation problem. A child with apraxia can exhibit the following characteristics ranging in severity from mild to severe:

- delayed expressive language development

- weakness of the lips, jaw, or tongue

- problems with fine motor movements

- problems with oral sensory perception (the child is unable to identify an object in her mouth by using the sense of touch)

Causes of Apraxia

Speech apraxia is a disorder based in a child's brain. Some children may have specific damage to a part of the brain detectable on an MRI (magnetic resonance imaging) brain scan. A child may be born with this damage or the damage may be the result of illness or an accident. However, for some children with apraxia, brain abnormalities cannot be detected. Recent studies have reported that this disorder also may be caused by a genetic link in some families. There are many factors that continue to be investigated to determine what might account for the variety of characteristics displayed by children who have apraxia.

DOMINICK AND THOMAS: APRAXIA

The next two profiles illustrate the signs and symptoms of apraxia in both a younger and an older child. The first is that of a younger child, Dominick. He is three years old and was recently diagnosed with apraxia. The second is that of Thomas, Dominick's older brother. He is seven years old and was diagnosed with apraxia several years ago. He participates in speech/language therapy three times a week.

As an infant, Dominick did not babble very much and he made very few consonantal sounds. Dominick said his first words at two years old and these words were not pronounced clearly and were missing sounds. Dominick can produce only a few consonant sounds: /b/, /p/, /m/, /t/, /d/, and /h/. He cannot copy mouth movement easily.

Thomas's understanding of language is more developed than his limited use of words would suggest. He uses a lot of pantomime and gestures to communicate. Thomas has difficulty imitating speech, and his speech production errors are highly inconsistent because sounds he uses in some words are omitted from others. He has more difficulty saying longer phrases than shorter phrases. Errors are noticed in his production of vowels, as well as consonants. Thomas often simplifies words by deleting consonants or vowels, and/or replaces difficult phonemes with easy ones. The rhythm of Thomas's speech is often inappropriate. This is because his speech is often slow, effortful, or halting. Sometimes he appears to struggle or use groping movements in order to make a sound. He may use either a real word or a nonsense word to convey another word. Thomas is very difficult to understand.

ORAL MOTOR PROBLEMS

Oral motor problems refer to the physical makeup of a person's mouth. *Oral motor development* refers to the ability to use the mouth properly.

The oral motor system is made up of many muscle groups that must have good tone, strength, and range of motion to control the tongue, lips, cheeks, and jaw. Clear speech depends on a person's ability to physically use her mouth properly and perform precise coordinated movements. If a child has difficulty with these muscles or the sensory aspects of the oral motor system, she may have difficulty making some sounds.

For example, if your child's tongue is too weak to reach the top of her mouth, she may have difficulty saying /r/ or /l/ sounds. If she can't feel or sense where in her mouth her tongue is touching, she cannot place her tongue behind her top teeth in order to produce the /t/ or /d/ sounds.

Eating Habits

If your child often chews with her mouth overstuffed with food, this may indicate that she cannot sense her mouth is full, and she may have poor control over the muscles of her oral motor system. If these kinds of eating habits continue over time, children do not learn to guide food between the chewing surfaces of their teeth and this, in turn, does not allow them to develop precise control of their tongue muscles.

ELAINE: ORAL MOTOR PROBLEMS

The next profile outlines some behavioral characteristics of Elaine, who is three and one-half years old and has been diagnosed by a speech/language pathologist as having oral motor problems. Elaine likes to eat nonfood items, such as crayons or glue. She often appears to pocket food in her check, and doesn't empty her mouth completely when swallowing. Elaine has difficulty licking food from her lips and puckering her lips. Her poor lip strength and control are apparent. Her productions of /p/, /b/, and /m/ are weak. Elaine's tongue has limited strength and coordination. She has poor production of sounds requiring an elevated tongue, such as /t/, /d/, /n/, and /l/. She also has poor production of some vowel sounds. Her voice sounds hypernasal, or as if air is coming out of her nose, rather than her mouth. This causes her productions of /p/, /b/, /s/, /z/, and /sh/ to be weak.

Tongue Thrust

Nearly all infants thrust or push their tongues forward when they swallow, instead of back. However, by the time a child reaches her sixth birthday, she should have instinctively changed to a normal swallowing pattern, which involves squeezing the tongue against the roof of the mouth instead of pushing the tongue forward. If a child does not develop a normal swallowing pattern, she may protrude her tongue between her teeth when she speaks or swallows, and when her tongue is at rest. This continuously exerts pressure against the structure of her mouth. As a result, her front teeth may push forward into an abnormal position and cause an open bite or a gapping between the teeth.

ARTICULATION PROBLEMS

Children who have a tongue-thrust-swallow pattern are more likely to have articulation problems than children who have developed a normal swallowing pattern (Casteel, Fletcher, and Bradley 1961). Other problems that might occur that may affect articulation include the following:

- high-arched palate

- muscles of the lips and nose become too relaxed

- jaws become misaligned and the lower jaw tends to fall back from the upper jaw

Evaluation and treatment of a tongue thrust usually involves many professionals and is tailored to a child's individual needs. For example, the speech/language pathologist doing the therapy will usually collaborate with an orthodontist, pediatric dentist, or other dentists, and with a medical specialist, including an ear, nose, and throat doctor.

GAVIN: TONGUE THRUST

This next profile outlines Gavin's speech characteristics. Gavin is eight years old and is currently in speech therapy working to correct his tongue thrust. He is currently being treated by an ear, nose, and throat doctor for allergies and has a past medical history of enlarged tonsils and adenoids. Gavin sucked his thumb until he was six years old. Gavin maintains an open mouth posture. His tongue pushes through his teeth during speech, especially on the /s/ and /z/ sounds. He tends to rest his tongue on his bottom lip, and when he swallows, he displays a noticeable tightening of his face and lip muscles.

SUMMING IT UP

Many factors can affect a child's ability to produce speech sounds correctly. Sometimes, the cause or causes of a child's articulation problem are easy to discover. Observation, formal and informal testing, and a review of your child's past medical and developmental history may help a speech/language pathologist discover why she isn't developing articulation skills as her peers do. However, in many cases, there seems to be no reason why a child doesn't talk as well as her age peers. In most cases, if a child is having articulation difficulties, intervening early is the most important step to help her learn to talk.

4

Language Development: Understanding and Using Words

People convey information and exchange messages by communication. Articulation disorders are the primary focus of this book, but learning to say sounds correctly is only one part of learning to communicate. Your child must also learn language to understand others and be able to express her own ideas, thoughts, and feelings. Speaking, reading, writing, gesturing, listening, and watching are all parts of language development. If you know the rules that govern how the words or symbols of a language are arranged, you can communicate using sentences you have never heard and understand sentences you have never spoken.

It's important to know about communication difficulties that may coexist with a child's articulation problems because a child who has a speech problem also may have difficulty developing language skills or may stutter (have difficulty with the rhythm and flow of speech). For example, in one study, researchers found that of 262 children with a fluency disorder, 42 percent had other suspected disabilities. The suspected areas of difficulty included language disorders, phonological disorders, and learning and reading disabilities (Arndt and Healey 2001).

We all know that children display a lot of variation as to when they say their first words, as well as in how many words they can say at two years old. This chapter outlines what most children do at specific ages, and explains how you can join in the fun of helping your young child learn to talk. If you have questions about your child's development at any age, it is always wise to seek professional help. Early identification and treatment of a problem can strengthen communication skills and enhance learning.

LANGUAGE IS MORE THAN WORDS

Your child's development of language is an important step in the development of her ability to learn and think, and will have a significant impact on her overall education. When a child enters school, she needs to be able to both understand others and express herself to succeed at new tasks like reading and writing. This is so because learning to read and write begins with oral speech. Your child learns to organize and focus her thoughts by talking about herself and her experiences. Children who are good listeners and speakers often become strong readers and writers. Children who are slow to learn to speak and understand language also may be slow at learning how a letter represents a sound, and may have difficulty making sense of what they read (Menyuk et al. 1991).

In order to understand and use language, we must have receptive and expressive skills.

Receptive Language

The ability to understand what we hear and see is called a *receptive language* skill. Children build their understanding of words by listening to people talking around them and by talking to them. Before children can say words themselves, they must develop receptive language skills, that is, connect meaning to objects and actions. The normal age span at which most children begin to understand words spoken to them is around six to nine months. Words are not learned in isolation but as part of the total flow of phrases and sentences. Children understand new words by building on the words they already know. Here's an example of a three-year-old child using her receptive language skills:

Mother: Amanda, please bring me the book.

Amanda picks the book up from the table and brings it to her mother.

Expressive Language

The way in which we express our thoughts and feelings, relate events, and answer questions is called *expressive language*. It includes choosing words with the correct meaning, as well as tone of voice, types of gestures, and the rate of speed used when we speak. Most babies learn quickly that communicating is a powerful tool that brings many exciting results. They use crying, sounds, and gestures to communicate before they begin to use words. The normal age range at which most children begin to use actual words is between nine and fifteen months. The average age is around fourteen months. Here's an example of a fifteen-month-old child using her expressive language skills:

Father: Amy, do you want more juice?

Amy: Juice.

Important Language Skills

At one year, most children say their first "showstopping" word, and a few years later many can ask and answer questions, tell stories, and speak logically. To do this, most children master many of the specific language skills discussed below during a relatively short time. However, if a child has difficulty in one or many of these areas, it may hinder her language development.

Phonology: This refers to the ability to learn the sound system of language and the rules that govern how those sounds combine to convey meaning (see chapter 1).

Semantics: This refers to both the ability to understand the meaning of words and to express words to convey meaning.

Morphology: This refers to the ability to understand and express the individual elements of a language, such as a root word, a prefix, or a suffix. Examples include /s/ added to the end of a word to express a plural (hat and hats); or /ed/ added to the end of a verb to express past tense (walk and walked).

Syntax: This refers to the ability to learn grammar or the rules that govern sentence construction, including word order and how to ask a question.

Pragmatics: These refer to the rules that govern language use in social situations. They include the ability to understand and follow the rules of conversation and how to interact with others. We are often judged not only on what we say, but also on how and when we choose to say it. Learning the rules of language use includes maintaining eye contact, taking turns to speak, keeping the needs of the listener in mind when speaking, understanding facial expressions, and responding appropriately when someone communicates with us.

Sequencing and organizing: These refer to the ability to understand the order of information. This enables us to plan and organize our ideas and to follow instructions.

Memory: This refers to the ability to remember the vocabulary and other language skills we have already mastered. Also, we must remember what others have said so that we can respond appropriately.

When and How Language Skills Develop

To understand speech development, researchers have studied when and how language skills develop in children. The predictable steps most children follow while learning to talk is the "how" or the development sequence. There is little variation in the "how" because most children tend to develop language skills in a predictable order.

For example, a child usually can express at least fifty single words before she can put two words together to form a short phrase.

The "when," or developmental milestones, are the behaviors most normally developing children are likely to display at approximately the same age. Since many factors can affect language learning, either slowing it down or enhancing it, the "when" can vary significantly.

Because of the huge variation in what is considered normal, children who are not quite "on schedule" are not necessarily delayed; instead they may be following their individual internal timetables. A young child's understanding and expression of words should grow and develop on a continuous basis. An indication for immediate concern would include any loss of language or social skills at any age.

EXERCISE 6: Developmental Milestones

To roughly assess your child's language development, read each developmental milestone listed below that applies to your child's age. Start at the lower end of the age range. For example, if your child has just turned two, review the guidelines for the eighteen months to two-year-old level and then review the two- to three-year-old guidelines. It's important to answer "always" or "sometimes" for each skill in the appropriate age range within a reasonable amount of time. If you have any concerns, see chapter 8.

BIRTH TO SIX MONTHS

My child turns her head when she hears my voice or other sounds, and she seems to be aware of people and objects in her environment.   Always _____ Sometimes _____ Never _____

My child enjoys social games like peekaboo and patty-cake. Always _____ Sometimes _____ Never _____

My child babbles when spoken to or smiled at. (*Babbling* is vocal play or the sounds babies make when they combine a consonant and a vowel and repeat the same syllable over and over again. *Examples:* "dada" and "baba.") Always _____ Sometimes _____ Never _____

SIX TO TWELVE MONTHS

My child clearly indicates a desire for an object.
Always _____ Sometimes _____ Never _____

My child imitates new sounds and actions.
Always _____ Sometimes _____ Never _____

My child appears to understand common words.
Always _____ Sometimes _____ Never _____

My child points or gestures. (Gestures may include waving good-bye or lifting her arms when she wants to be picked up.)
Always _____ Sometimes _____ Never _____

My child imitates speech sounds and uses sounds to get my attention.   Always _____ Sometimes _____ Never _____

My child looks at the person talking to her and shows interest and an intention to communicate. (Infants might use gestures and sounds to direct an adult to an object they want.)
Always _____ Sometimes _____ Never _____

TWELVE TO EIGHTEEN MONTHS

My child uses a wide range of speech sounds in her babbling and jargoning. (The early true language sounds that children make by putting together different vowels and consonant combinations and using real tones and inflections are called *jargoning*. *Example:* "badaga?")
Always _____ Sometimes _____ Never _____

My child tries to imitate and produce single words.
Always _____ Sometimes _____ Never _____

My child can express ten meaningful words.
Always _____ Sometimes _____ Never _____

My child understands at least fifty words.
Always _____ Sometimes _____ Never _____

My child is continuously understanding and expressing new words.   Always _____ Sometimes _____ Never _____

My child can follow simple requests, such as "Look at the dog."
Always _____ Sometimes _____ Never _____

My child can respond to simple questions by answering yes or no. *Example:* "Do you want some more juice?"
Always _____ Sometimes _____ Never _____

My child shows an interest in pictures.
Always _____ Sometimes _____ Never _____

EIGHTEEN TO TWENTY-FOUR MONTHS

My child speaks at least fifty words.
Always _____ Sometimes _____ Never _____

My child is beginning to use two-word combinations. *Examples:* "More milk" and "My turn."
Always _____ Sometimes _____ Never _____

My child can follow simple, one-step requests, like "Please get the book."
Always _____ Sometimes _____ Never _____

TWENTY-FOUR TO THIRTY-SIX MONTHS

My child has a vocabulary of fifty or more clear words or word approximations, and she is learning to engage in short dialogues.
Always _____ Sometimes _____ Never _____

My child asks simple questions and responds to simple questions with yes and no.   Always _____ Sometimes _____ Never _____

My child understands simple stories and conversations, and uses three to four words together, like "my big bear."
Always _____ Sometimes _____ Never _____

My child asks and answers what and who questions. *Examples:* "What are you doing?" and "Who is on the porch?"
Always _____ Sometimes _____ Never _____

My child initiates conversations.
Always _____ Sometimes _____ Never _____

THREE TO FOUR YEARS OLD

My child uses sentences that are well formed.
Always _____   Sometimes _____   Never _____

My child responds to simple two-step directions. *Example:* "Go upstairs and get your blue coat."
Always _____   Sometimes _____   Never _____

My child likes to listen to two or three lines of a story and can answer simple questions about what was read.
Always _____   Sometimes _____   Never _____

My child understands almost all of what is said to her.
Always _____   Sometimes _____   Never _____

FOUR TO FIVE YEARS OLD

My child asks questions with proper word order. *Example:* "Where is my ball?"
Always _____   Sometimes _____   Never _____

My child uses the prepositions "on," "in" and "under."
Always _____   Sometimes _____   Never _____

My child is beginning to use past tense verbs. *Example:* "He walked."   Always _____   Sometimes _____   Never _____

My child can recite and sing simple songs and rhymes.
Always _____   Sometimes _____   Never _____

My child speaks in four- to five-word sentences.
Always _____   Sometimes _____   Never _____

My child can follow a series of three directions. *Example:* "Please get the dog's bowl and his leash and bring them to the back porch."   Always _____   Sometimes _____   Never _____

My child takes part in conversations with other children.
Always _____   Sometimes _____   Never _____

My child speaks clearly enough for adults outside the home to understand her.   Always _____   Sometimes _____   Never _____

FIVE YEARS AND OLDER

Most five- and six-year-old children are able to understand language and communicate in a clear and logical manner with adults and peers in many different situations. Schaefer and DiGeronimo (2000) state that most six-year-old children can express about 2,500 words, and their average sentence uses seven words. At this point, most children begin to use their language skills to learn to read, write, and spell. They can follow a teacher's instructions, listen to stories, answer questions, and use simple reasoning. You should be able to have a reasonably meaningful conversation with your child about past and future events that relate to her daily life. At this age, most children are using language to understand ideas and are learning to predict and draw conclusions.

Delayed Language Skill Development

If a child has a noticeable problem with understanding and/or expressing her thoughts, and her language skills are significantly behind those of her peers, she may have a language disorder. It is estimated that language disorders affect up to 3 percent of the preschool population and 1 percent of children in grades one through twelve (NIDCD 1995). Some language disorders have physical or known causes, such as hearing impairment. However, these difficulties sometimes appear without any known or physical cause. It's important to remember there are many normal variations in the production of speech sounds and how thoughts are put into words. These differences are considered a disorder when they interfere with our ability to understand others, express our own thoughts, and learn new concepts that are appropriate for our age.

CHARACTERISTICS OF A LANGUAGE DISORDER

A language disorder can involve both receptive and expressive language skills. How a language disorder affects a child's social and academic skills depends on many factors, including the areas of language affected, how severe the deficit is, the skills and strengths the child has in other areas, and the child's self-confidence and self-esteem.

A child who has a language disorder may exhibit one or a combination of the following characteristics:

- She may use few words to communicate and have a difficult time retrieving the words she wants to say. When asked a question, she answers in one or two words and is unable to elaborate or extend her answer. She may rarely ask questions. She may let adults do most of the talking. When asked a question, she answers in short phrases and is unable to elaborate or add additional information.

- She may have difficulty understanding and using concept words. These are the words that describe position (in, on, under), time (before, after, first), quality (big, old, hot), and quantity (more, some, less). She is unable to follow directions.

- She may have difficulty understanding questions or following other people's conversations. This may be because she understands only part of the messages or is unable to pick out the important words. For example, when asked, "Where do you live?" She may respond, "I have a dog."

- She may use related or incorrect words to express her thoughts. She may substitute different words with related meanings (clock for watch). She may substitute similar-sounding words (knock for knob); substitute visually related words (cake for cupcake); talk around words—for example, instead of saying "in my desk," she might say, "the place where I put my pencil," or she may often insert long pauses between her words and sentences.

- She may not have learned the rules of grammar. She often eliminates small words, such as "in" and "on" and uses pronouns and verbs incorrectly. *Example:* "Me likes it," instead of "I like candy."

- She may have difficulty understanding and using social rules of conversation and interactions. For example, she may have difficulty taking turns or maintaining eye contact during conversation, or cannot extend a conversation.

PREPARING YOUR CHILD FOR SUCCESS IN SCHOOL

When your child begins school, age-appropriate social and emotional maturity and well-developed language skills will contribute to her success. New and different communication demands will be placed on her when she enters school. To foster a love of learning that will last forever, give her the tools she needs to succeed.

Help Your Child Learn to Follow Directions

Preschool students are often greeted with these kinds of directions: "Good morning. Put your coat in the closet, get a drink, and then come sit with me on the carpet for story time."

Children must listen to learn and learn to listen. For a child to follow directions, she must understand the meaning of the words and remember the directions while she acts on the request. Therefore, give your child directions at her level of understanding. Most one- to two-year-old children can follow a simple one-step direction that contains words they already understand. *Examples:* "Come here" or "Get your coat." By two to three years of age, most children can follow a simple two-step direction, such as, "Get your doll and bring it to me." Around three to five years, children can respond to a variety of two-step directions and even some three-step directions. *Example:* "Touch your nose, clap your hands, and then stand up."

EXERCISE 7: Developing Your Child's Listening Skills

The following suggestions may help your child learn to follow directions:

Make every attempt to keep background noise to a minimum. When you begin a conversation or give instructions, turn off the TV, radio, and other noise sources or lower them so your child can focus on your words without hearing competing noises.

Get your child's attention. Call her name or use some other attention-getter before you begin to speak, and wait until she is looking at you. Stand as close to her as possible. By helping her to develop the habit of looking at the person who is speaking, she will learn to absorb visual cues that will help her to understand what is being said. Speak clearly and slowly, and use gestures like pointing to objects or locations.

Check with your child to see if she has understood important information or instructions. Instead of asking, "Do you understand?" ask her to repeat or explain what you've said or have asked her to do. If she didn't understand the first time you said the directions, paraphrase the instructions and information into shorter and simpler sentences rather than repeating the same words.

Use chunking. If you are giving your child more than one direction, it is best to say the related directions together and then pause before giving the next direction. This useful technique is called *chunking*. *Example:* "Brush your teeth and wash your hands." (Pause) "Next, please get my glasses on my dresser and bring them downstairs to me." Rather than: "Go upstairs and brush your teeth, please get my glasses on my dresser, and wash your hands too."

Speak in a way your child can understand. The vocabulary and sentence structure you use should be appropriate to your child's age. You can refer to the guidelines above about how children learn to follow directions. Also, accent key words by stretching them out, pronouncing them slightly louder, or pausing after them.

Use gamelike activities to develop your three- to six-year-old child's listening skills.

- **At the supermarket:** Ask your child to follow simple directions. *Example:* "Please get three cans of chicken noodle soup."

- **Play games while riding in the car.** *Examples:* Say three or more words that go together and one that doesn't belong. Ask which word doesn't belong and why. Use places, colors, days of the week, shapes, tools, toys, and so forth.

- **Say a series of three to five words or number words.** Ask your child, "What did I say first?" "What did I say last?" "What did I say after [or before] _____ ?"

- **Say a series of five or six words.** Ask your child to clap when she hears the name of a food, animal, place, and so on.

- **Play "Today I saw a _____ ."** Have your child repeat what you said and add the name of another person, place, or thing. Continue the game by taking turns repeating the sentence and adding a word to the list.

- **Play fill in the missing letters or numbers.** For example, say "A, B, blank, D"; "5, 6, blank, blank."

Help Your Child Learn to Make Choices

Having the opportunity to make their own decisions and choices is essential to children's development. At playtime, preschoolers are often asked questions like, "Do you want to play in the blocks area or the kitchen center?" Sometimes, children brought up in homes where parents makes all the choices for them cannot make important choices on their own.

For a child, the first step in making reasonable choices is to understand how things in her environment are the same and how they are different. By listening to you describe objects, events, and people, your child will begin to understand and express words that tell about the important details in her world. This will enable her to make and express reasonable choices. Talk about color, shape, and size; how objects feel; and the sounds you hear as you go about your daily life activities.

Build Your Child's Knowledge of Words

When listening to a story, preschool students are often asked questions like these: "Do you know what this is? Did you ever see anything that looked like this?" Your child will learn new words by listening to you explaining things in her natural environment as you go about your daily life activities. Encourage her to ask you about any new words she hears. Talk about a difficult word and what it means. Use difficult words in a sentence and encourage her to do the same.

WORD ASSOCIATIONS

As your child learns the names of objects, she must also begin to make associations and link new information to the words she already knows. She will do this by learning to classify objects and mentally placing them in groups or categories. The categories into which your child divides her world will continually change as she continues to learn new words.

CLASSIFYING WORDS

Give your child collections of safe objects she can classify. Talk about how they are the same and how they are different. When it is time to clean up, help her put all the stuffed animals on the top shelf, the toy cars on the middle shelf, and the things that are round on the bottom shelf. On trips to the supermarket, talk about the groups or categories you see: for example, fruits, vegetables, and drinks.

Help Your Child Learn How to Have a Conversation

Preschool students are often asked questions about special events that may have happened at home. For example, "What did you do at your grandmother's house yesterday?" To encourage your child to carry on a conversation with you, give her time to express herself or tell you what happened. For example, try not to put words into her mouth too quickly; instead, gently guide her when she seems unable to continue. By adding related information, you may help her stay on topic and extend her conversation.

COMMENTING ON YOUR CHILD'S SPEECH

Show that you are listening by commenting on something she just said. It is also important to respond to your child's intended message rather than correct her speech production or grammar. Try providing an appropriate model by repeating her words in your response. For example, if your child says, "I wunned weally fast," you might say, "Oh you ran really fast in the park. What did you do next?" Encourage your child to restate an unclear word or sentence. You might say, "Did you mean _____ ?"

ASKING QUESTIONS

To keep the conversation going, it is best to focus on asking your child what, why, which, and how questions, rather than who and what. Give her choices. *Example:* "Which did you like better, the ice cream or going to see the animals?" If you ask only "Did you have fun at Grandmom's house?" the verbal exchange is over when she answers "Yes!"

USING DIFFERENT KINDS OF LANGUAGE

Try to increase your child's use of different kinds of language, such as commenting, requesting, and questioning. Take advantage of naturally occurring interactions. For example, practice greetings at the beginning and end of the day, let your child ask other family members what they would like for dessert, or have her ask for needed materials while doing an art project.

Help Your Child Learn About Time and How It Passes

Preschool students are often told things like, "After we clean up the block area, your mom will be here." Your child's concept of time will develop slowly, as most children live in the here and now, and they become concerned with time only when they must wait for something.

When you explain what comes first or talk about what happened yesterday, you will help her begin to understand what time is and how it passes. Often use words and phrases like these: next, after, before, yesterday, today, tomorrow, next week.

EXERCISE 8: Developing Your Child's Understanding of Time

1. Give your child a simple chore such as clearing away her toys or feeding a pet. Help her look at the clock when she begins and again when she is finished. Talk about how the hands of the clock have moved and how time has passed.

2. As you tuck her into bed, ask her to tell you about something she did in the morning, afternoon, or evening.

3. Make a chain before your child's birthday or special holiday. As each day passes, remove one link. Talk about how many days have passed and how many days there still are before the big event.

4. Translate time into something your child can see by displaying a large calendar. Let her draw pictures in the empty spaces to signify special activities or events. Your child will soon learn to see that yesterday came before today and tomorrow comes after today.

5. Talk to her as you organize, or perform a simple activity to help her learn to plan, organize, and explain what has happened, will happen, or what she wants to happen. Use words that describe order often: *Examples:* first, next, and last.

    ■   First, I will let the cake cool.

    ■   Next, we will put the icing on the cake.

    ■   Last, we will eat it.

6. Throughout the day, ask your child silly questions about sequenced events that are performed often:

- "Do we pay for the groceries before we buy them?"

- "Do you put your socks on after you put on your new shoes?"

- "Do we turn on the TV after you watch it?"

- "Do we read a story after we go to sleep?"

5 Read to Speak: Literacy and Articulation

Learning to read and write begins with your child's development of articulation and language skills. It is believed that the age at which a child learns the alphabet, or even the methods by which he is taught to read in school, are not as important as the skills he gains from pre-reading activities early in life.

It is important for every child, especially those who may be having a hard time learning to talk, to develop an early enjoyment of spoken and written language. It is never too early or too late to begin the activities recommended below. These suggested activities may give your child the tools and motivation he needs to read when he is developmentally ready. In this chapter, you will discover many important things you can do create a "literacy-rich" environment for your child. A child who lives in a literacy-rich environment has many opportunities to:

- listen to books read aloud

- engage in one-on-one conversations with caring adults

- talk about books—discussing the characters, actions, and plot

- engage in pretend play

- be exposed to many different reading and writing materials

TALK, TALK, TALK

The size of your child's vocabulary is a strong predictor of reading success. One reason children do not become proficient readers is because they don't have a functional vocabulary that enables them to understand the words they read (Ediger 1999).

Scientific research has found that the more language your child hears and the more responsive you are to his communications—even his earliest babbling sounds—the more his inborn ability to acquire language will be enhanced. The natural way for your child to learn the meaning of words is to listen to you talk in relation to the daily events going on around you. In this way, he learns to associate the words you say with the actions, objects, or thoughts you describe.

Using Daily Routine Activities

You can expose your child to a large number and variety of words by making talking a part of everything you and your child do together. To a young child, the whole world is new and even the most routine activities are learning experiences. Just remember to follow his lead and be a good listener. Try the suggestions below, and you will soon learn to recognize the hundreds of opportunities that each day offers to introduce your child to new words.

BUILDING YOUR CHILD'S VOCABULARY

- Questions, answers, and comments: Excursions to the zoo, aquarium, supermarket, or post office should always be accompanied by lots of questions, answers, and comments.

- Doing, seeing, feeling, and touching: Talk to your child about what you're doing, seeing, feeling, and touching while you cook dinner, vacuum the carpet, set the table, or simply pour your child a drink. As you name and describe different objects, you can increase your child's knowledge of their different characteristics; for example, you can name their colors, shapes, sizes, and textures.

- Use specific words: Making only slight changes in the way you speak to your child can make a large difference in his vocabulary development, too. Instead of saying, "I will cut the sandwich for you," try saying, "I will cut the sandwich in half for you." Instead of, "We will be there soon," try saying, "We will be there in two hours."

- Ask questions: Asking your child questions is a great way to develop his ability to learn, think, and explain, while practicing talking. Try not to always ask questions that require a one-word answer or a yes or no response. If you ask your child, "Did you have fun in school today" the conversational exchange is over and done with when he says yes or no.

One- and two-year-olds are usually able to answer simple yes or no questions and respond appropriately to "What's this?"

Two- and three-year-olds may enjoy answering simple questions: who, what, why, and what do you do with a _____ ? Fill in the blank and keep changing it.

Three- and four-year-olds can answer questions that have more than one answer. These questions often begin with "how" and "what if" and require a child to think for himself. For example, "How do you know it is going to rain?" or "What would happen if the ball hit the car?" Most children at this age are also learning to answer how many, how much, and which questions. For example, "How many boxes do you have?" or "Which one is bigger?"

EXERCISE 9: Errands as Learning Tools

As you will see, there is no need to buy expensive equipment or sit at the kitchen table with flash cards to build a young child's vocabulary. Instead, let the activities in your daily routine become your child's learning tools. Ask yourself these questions:

While driving, do you silently plan your day? If your answer is yes, try this instead: Open your dialogue by saying your child's name or some attention-getting word, such as "Look," because sitting in the front seat driving, with your child secured in the back seat, doesn't allow you to establish eye contact. Talk about the variety of sights and sounds you see and hear as you drive. *Examples:* "See the blue house?" or "Listen to the siren." Ask your preschool child to find things that are red, round, or square. Find numbers or letters on signs and billboards. Recite nursery rhymes, count out loud, or sing his favorite song. Or, simply talk to him about an upcoming or favorite family event.

At the supermarket, do you silently push your cart through the aisles as your child sits in the cart facing you? If your answer is yes, try the following suggestions instead. (Would you like to sit in a chair facing a familiar adult who has nothing to say?) Name the items as you pass by them or put them in your cart. Count the potatoes as you put them in the bag. Talk about colors, shapes, and sizes. Compare the sizes of boxes and bags as you make choices. Talk about how items are the same and how they are different. *Examples:* "This bag is heavy." and "This bag is light." Talk about how the supermarket is arranged by categories (fruits, vegetables, paper products, breakfast foods). Learning about categories helps children learn to link new words to information they already know.

Do you bathe and dress your child silently? If your answer is yes, instead try talking about body parts, kinds of clothes, and where they go: "Shoes go on your feet after your socks." Talk about how clothing feels: "soft sweater and rough jeans." Give simple directions to help your child learn about spatial concepts. *Examples:* "Tilt your head back." or "Put your head through the neck hole of your new sweater."

Do you prepare dinner silently? If your answer is yes, try this instead: To help your child learn about the logical order of events, talk about what you will do first and what you will do after that. *Example:* "First, I will put the butter in the bowl; next you can help me stir the batter." Talk about what you are doing to help build your child's knowledge of actions words. *Example:* "I am pouring the batter." "I am opening the oven door." Talk about "how many" or "how much" to teach your child about quantity. *Examples:* "two eggs" or "a box of raisins." Read a recipe aloud and let your child help you follow the directions.

READ, READ, READ

Reading aloud is a great way to spend quality time with your child and develop an important foundation for the development of his speech and language skills. Story time provides many opportunities for emphasizing sounds, intonation patterns, and word meanings. When you read a book or recite a rhyme to a young child at any age, you enhance his visual and listening abilities and increase his vocabulary. Children learn how sounds are sequenced together to represent word meanings and how to say sounds by listening to them repeated many, many times. When you are reading aloud, your child is listening to you model how to produce sounds in words, phrases, and sentences.

Begin Early

Infancy is the perfect time to begin to read aloud to your child. Even though at first he will not understand the meaning of your words, researchers have found that he is learning and remembering the rhythm and inflections of how the language spoken around him is organized. Patricia Kuhl, a professor of speech and hearing sciences at the University of Washington at Seattle, together with her colleagues found that infants map the sound structure of their native language (1992).

By six months, babies recognize individual vowels and consonants, and by nine months, they recognize the pattern of words. Your baby's developing brain needs a steady stream of stimuli to learn to process sounds and shape his babbling into words. The United States Department of Education publication *Ready, Set, Read* (Korelek 1997) tells us that if you begin to read to your child daily in his infancy, by the time he is five years old, he will have been fed roughly nine hundred hours of brain food!

NEWBORNS

Even though your newborn can't understand what actual words mean yet, he listens to you read and learns to hear the differences between sounds in words, recognize where words begin and end, and understand the rhythm and inflections of the language spoken around him. Hold your infant in your arms and read to him. It doesn't matter what you read. You can read your favorite novel, your shopping list, or the daily newspaper. As your child begins to associate words with physical closeness, he will learn to love hearing your voice, watching your face, and looking at colorful pictures.

Developmental highlights: Kids this age love books that use simple, bright illustrations, especially when you use an animated tone of voice and lots of hand gestures while reading. When choosing a book for a very young child, experts suggest simple but brightly illustrated books constructed of cloth or cardboard, such as *Pat the Bunny*, by Dorothy Kunhardt (2000).

If you choose books with not much text but they illustrate objects and actions familiar to your child, you may hold his attention longer. Use animated gestures, high-pitched tones, and speed up and slow down your tempo to keep him interested. You may recall that part of the joy of hearing *Goldilocks and the Three Bears* read aloud was hearing Papa Bear's deep gruff voice, Mamma Bear's high-pitched voice, and Baby Bear's soft, sweet, childlike voice.

TWO TO FIVE MONTHS

Developmental highlights: Kids this age love rhyme, repetition, and reading games. Around the age of two to five months, your baby may enjoy hearing books with lots of rhyme and repetition, such as *Berenstains' B Book*, by Stan and Jan Berenstain (1997) or *Each Peach Pear Plum*, by Allan and Janet Ahlberg (1999). This is a good time to take advantage of the child's growing curiosity by playing games while you read aloud. Run two fingers up your child's arms as you recite, "Hickory dickory dock, the mouse ran up the clock."

SEVEN TO TWELVE MONTHS

Developmental highlights: Kids of this age love holding and touching books with lots of shapes and textures. So, between seven and nine months is a great time to introduce books with different shapes and textures for your child to touch and hold. Encourage him to imitate the way you handle and touch these books. Around twelve months, encourage him to imitate the words while you are reading. Ask him to show you an object or action on the page. After he points to the picture, slowly repeat the word several times and encourage him to say it. Most one-year-old children enjoy books about animals, cars, trucks, and other children.

TODDLERS

Developmental highlights: Choose the time to read aloud wisely. Although kids this age love concept books, nursery rhymes, and books with hidden objects, many toddlers are often working on their movement skills, and sitting still may not be first on their list of things to do. Therefore, to make reading a more pleasurable experience for both of you, you must choose the time carefully. Good times to read aloud are often before naps or bedtime, when your child's energy level is slightly lower.

Let your child pick the book and choose the place where he wants to read it. Hold his attention longer by choosing books that have colorful pictures, objects he can touch and feel, or objects he can find hidden under a flap, such as, *Where's Spot,* by Eric Hill (2003).

At this stage of development, experts also recommend concept books, such as ABC and counting books, or books where your child can anticipate what will happen next. The rhymes of traditional nursery rhymes, such as in Mother Goose books, usually appeal to toddlers too. Allow your child to handle the pages and turn them only when he is ready. As he handles books and explores their sizes, shapes, and details by himself, he is becoming an independent reader and soon may begin choosing books on his own.

Practice talking about the pictures, rather than actually reading the words on the page. It is now well understood that reading a story aloud has a greater influence on literary development when the child has an opportunity to talk about the story. When you point to the pictures, talk about them in relation to an event or an object in your child's world. *Example:* "See the ball? Your ball is on the top shelf in the garage." Compare objects in the book with familiar objects in his environment. *Example:* "The dog is big, just like our dog, Bandit."

While you describe the colors, shapes, and sizes you are looking at, your child is listening and processing your sounds and words.

PRESCHOOLERS

Developmental highlights: Kids this age are learning to choose their own books, and they enjoy books that mirror their own experiences. By the age of three, most children can follow a simple story line and will understand and remember many ideas presented in simple storybooks. Now you can enjoy conversing with your child about the stories you are reading.

Establish a special time to read as well as special places to store children's books in your home. Your child should be able to reach the books and get them himself. Try to read when he asks for a story. That reinforces the idea that reading is important. If you can't stop what you are doing immediately, suggest that he look at the book himself while he waits for you. As a special treat, fill a bag with books by a favorite author (Dr. Seuss), on a theme (animals), or that emphasize particular sounds. For easy access, place the bag near a rocking chair or favorite reading area. Bring the bag along when you leave home so you can read together while waiting at the doctor's office or on a park bench.

Your child may enjoy choosing books at the local library about experiences he has had or is going to have, such as a trip to the zoo, an airplane ride, or the arrival of a new sibling.

EXERCISE 10:
Encouraging Toddlers to Read

Talk about the story. Talk about the story while you read it or later in the day to help develop your child's ability to recall important information. Stress words that tell about time and cause and effect ("next," "before," "because," "since," and so forth).

Give your child many opportunities to practice talking. Ask him questions about the characters and his favorite part of the story. As he begins to understand why things happen, stop before the end of the story and ask him to guess what might happen next and why he thinks this will happen. Ask questions like "What do you think the girl will do next?" "How do you think the doggy feels?" or "Where do you think the kitten is hiding?"

Reinforce the concepts and vocabulary. Before or after reading a story, reinforce the concepts and vocabulary in your child's natural environment. For example, before reading *If You Give a Moose a Muffin*, by Laura Joffe Numeroff (1995), bake muffins together. Eat a muffin at an appropriate time during the story. *The Mitten: A Ukrainian Folktale*, by Jan Brett (1996), is a story about a group of animals that find shelter inside a lost mitten. After reading this childhood favorite, help your child discover how many of his toy animals or small objects he can fit into his own mitten. Talk about whether his mitten holds more or less than the mitten in the story. Try using a grown-up's glove and see what happens.

Simple words and short sentences. Read books that use simple words and short sentences. Follow the print with your finger and sometimes point back and forth between the printed word and a picture of the object that it represents. Your child may soon learn to attend to individual words and to see how one spoken word corresponds to a combination of letters. Soon, he may begin to recognize letters of the alphabet, whole words, punctuation marks, and the connections between printed and spoken words as he half-memorizes and half-recognizes the familiar words on the page.

Practice making speech sounds. Let your child practice making speech sounds by encouraging him to participate in reading predictable words in the text, or read a few words, then stop and let him fill in the blanks. *Example:* "The boy is sitting on the _____ ."
At first, point to the picture, such as a swing. The next time you read the story (which may be in a few minutes if it's a favorite), try saying the phrase with the blank and see if he can say the word without your pointing cue.

TELL YOUR CHILD STORIES

Regardless of your child's age, simply telling him a story is a great time to emphasize sounds. It can be as long or short as time permits, told anywhere, and tailored to your child's experiences. Use new words to expand his vocabulary or emphasize a particular sound in your story-telling. For example, if your child is having trouble saying the /ch/ sound, make up a story about "Charlie and his choo choo train that carried chickens to China."

When you tell a story to a young child, you inspire him to create stories of his own, and you give him the opportunity to focus on and realize the power of words. Encourage him to tell you a story. Ask him questions to help him develop his ability to think and organize his thoughts, and let him know you are interested in what he tells you.

ENCOURAGE YOUR CHILD'S INTEREST IN THE WRITTEN WORD

Begin to encourage your child's interest in the printed word. When he is developmentally ready, it will be easier for him to learn how to recognize letters and eventually to read words.

EXERCISE 11: Expose Your Child to Words and Letters

- Write and say each letter of your child's name often.

- Ask your child to draw a picture. When he is finished, ask him to tell you about his drawing while you write the words he says on the bottom of the page.

- Have your child help you write a shopping list. Say the words aloud as you print them on the paper.

- Create a scrapbook together by cutting out pictures of people and places and labeling them. Label objects in your child's bedroom (door, bed, closet, and window). Use printed word cards. For added fun, make up a duplicate card and see if your child can find a word match. This will help him to realize that print conveys meaning and he will become aware of whole words.

- Create a special place where your child can read and write during playtime. Make or buy a child-size table or desk, low open shelves, a bulletin board, and a clothesline and clothespins for hanging up his artwork. Let him explore letters and numbers with alphabet and number magnets, sponges, or stamps and stamp pads. Give him materials to write with and on, such as chalk and a chalkboard, paint and brushes, paper and markers, or wax crayons.

DON'T STOP READING ALOUD

Jim Trelease, author of *The Read-Aloud Handbook* (2001), recommends that you should continue to read socially appropriate books aloud to your child long after he can read. According to researchers who study how children learn to listen, children listen at much higher comprehension levels than they read until around eighth grade. Therefore, first-graders can enjoy books written at the fourth-grade level, and fifth-graders can enjoy books written for seventh-grade reading levels, when the subject is appropriate and these books are read aloud to them. Reading stories to your child at his interest level, but beyond his reading level, not only may develop your child's vocabulary and pronunciation of more complex words and phrases, it also may instill a love of stories that will motivate him to become a lifelong reader.

Model Good Pronunciation

When your child is working on a particular sound in speech therapy or is unable to make a particular sound, emphasize this sound as you read the words in the text. Even though he may not be ready to make the correct production of the sound himself, he will be listening to you as you model the correct sound production, and he may begin to recognize the correct and incorrect productions of a troublesome sound.

LISTEN TO YOUR CHILD READ

Listening to your child read to you is just as important as reading aloud to him. Ask his teacher or school librarian to recommend books that are at his reading level and will showcase his developing skills at home. Try taking turns. First you read a paragraph and then have your child read the following one. Gradually, as he becomes a more fluent reader, try taking turns reading a full page. If he is not yet a fluent reader, this may help to keep the story interesting.

DECONSTRUCT DIFFICULT WORDS

When your child has trouble reading a word, help him use the skills he has learned about letters and sounds: take the word apart; talk about the beginning sound and ask, "Do you recognize any part of the word?" Tell your child to skip the difficult word and continue reading the sentence. Encourage him to think of a word that might make sense or to look at the illustrations for a clue to the pronunciation of the word. Always keep in mind that reading together should be fun, and it's not necessarily a time to "teach reading." If your child seems at all frustrated, bored, or tired, it's best to stop.

CHOOSE BOOKS THAT EMPHASIZE A TROUBLESOME SOUND

Some books contain a predominance of a particular sound and are helpful to children who have difficulty saying that sound. In chapter 7, you will find a list of recommended books that emphasize specific sounds. For example, *Carl Goes Shopping,* by Alexandra Day

(1992), contains many words that have the /sh/ sound in the beginning (shopping), middle (pushing), and final positions (fish) in words. Of course, you also can skim through the text of any book to determine if a particular sound is repeated often.

When you are reading to your child, you might ask him to touch his head when he hears an /s/ sound at the end of a word. If he is reading to you and he has progressed to the point where he is able to make a troublesome sound correctly in all positions of words while reading aloud, listen and praise him when he correctly says a word with this sound. One of the most important factors is for you to speak clearly and slowly and model the correct production of sounds for your child to hear.

Whether your child is talking about the pictures, filling in words, or reading the entire page to you, he may omit or substitute incorrect sounds. The printed words can help him understand why his production of a sound was not correct. Explain to him how the letters in the word he sees tell his mouth which sounds to make. If your child omits a sound, show him the printed word and point out the sounds that he didn't say in the word. For example, if he omits an ending sound and says "mou" instead of "mouse," show him the printed word and how mouse has an /s/ sound at the end. Model the correct pronunciation of "mouse." If he substitutes an incorrect sound, for example, "wabbit" instead of "rabbit," refer to the printed word and explain how "rabbit" begins with the /r/ sound, instead of the /w/ sound. Model the correct production of "rabbit," saying the /r/ sound louder and longer. Encourage your child to watch your lips and tongue while you make the sound.

SET A GOOD EXAMPLE

Many school-age children who are good readers had parents who set examples for them by reading themselves. It is well understood that when a parent puts the emphasis on reading as entertainment, rather than as a skill to be learned, the child develops a more positive attitude toward reading.

- Make frequent trips to the library to let him choose his own books, share your childhood favorites, and select books recommended by teachers and librarians.

- Show your child that words are everywhere. As you pass by stores, road signs, and billboards, read the words on the signs aloud.

- Play a board game together and read the directions out loud.

- Demonstrate how you use books, newspapers, and other print media to find out information and get things done every day: What time a movie starts; today's weather forecast; or how to travel to a new city.

6 Encouraging Your Child to Talk

This chapter will provide your child with many activities to hear how sounds are pronounced correctly and to practice talking. When we speak, we don't pause between the separate words; we talk in a steady stream using the sounds that form words. Sounds are seldom learned in isolation but as part of the words we hear. For some children, learning the difference between the correct and incorrect productions of a sound may be difficult. The activities in this chapter will enhance your child's ability to acquire new sounds when she is developmentally ready.

EXERCISE 12: Are You Helping Your Child Learn to Talk?

Review the following questions and answers, and take a close look at how you interact with your child.

1. Do you speak clearly, naturally, and, most of all, correctly? Yes _____ No _____

   Correct Answer: Yes. Take a close look at the way you interact with your child. Speaking clearly and naturally includes establishing eye contact, speaking at an easy-to-understand rate, and saying sounds precisely.

2.   Do you ask your child to repeat a word she has said incorrectly? Yes _____ No _____

Correct Answer: No. In most cases, it is wise not to ask your child to repeat a word after she has said it incorrectly. (Of course, if your child is participating in speech therapy, follow the speech/language pathologist's instructions.) Many children are not able to say a sound correctly because they do not hear the difference between the correct and incorrect production of the sound. Therefore, give your child many opportunities to hear the sound modeled (said) correctly. As you repeat the word, over-enunciate the sound your child is mispronouncing by saying it louder and longer. Continue talking and make the troublesome word a natural part of your conversation.

Incorrect Example

Child: Look at the dot.

Parent: It's not a dot.

Child: Yes, it is. Look at the dot. (Pointing to the dog.)

Parent: That's not how you say it.

This child is not getting an opportunity to hear the correct production of the error sound.

Correct Example

Child: I see a dot.

Parent: Yes, I see the doggg. He is a big doggg. Would you like a doggg like that?

Child: Yes, I want a dott.

Parent: Maybe we can get a doggg soon.

This parent gives her child many chances to hear how the sound is said correctly. She over-enunciates the /g/ sound and uses "dog" as part of the natural conversation.

3. Do you praise your child often?   Yes _____ No _____

Correct Answer: Yes. It's important to recognize your child's strengths often. Perhaps she can climb the jungle gym faster than all her friends, or she can build a fantastic castle with her Legos. Let her know that you are proud of her when she makes sounds correctly too. *Example:* "I like how you said look, not wook," rather than saying just, "Good talking." Your pleasure and excitement will motivate your child to speak and will also contribute to her self-esteem.

4. Do you pretend to understand your child even when you don't? Yes _____ No _____

Correct Answer: No. In most cases, it's best to gently tell your child that you are having trouble understanding what she is trying to tell you, rather than pretending to understand her words. Try to focus on what she says, rather than how she says it. Show by your words and actions that you are trying to understand. Try understanding just one word. Use that word to ask her questions. You might ask, "Can you help me understand, please?" If your child feels she needs to help you, and that you (not she) has a problem, she may repeat her words more slowly, try to say them another way, or point or use some sort of gesture to be your helper. Show your acceptance with nonverbal responses such as smiles, hugs, and friendly words.

5. Do you monitor your child for ear infections? Yes _____ No _____

Correct Answer: Yes. (See chapter 4 for signs and symptoms of ear infections.) If you suspect your child has an ear infection, call your physician immediately. If she does have an ear infection, remember to take her back to the doctor for a follow-up visit to make sure her hearing has returned to normal.

6. Do you listen and compare your child's speech to other children? Yes _____ No _____

Correct Answer: No. Many parents compare their child's speech development to that of other children in the family or neighborhood. However, even though some children can say speech sounds correctly at a very early age, others may be eight or nine before they can say all the sounds correctly. (See chapter 3.) If you have any questions about your child's development in any area at any age, it's always wise to seek professional help.

7. Do you educate others about your child's speech difficulties?
    Yes ____ No ____

    Correct Answer: Yes. Of course, you would never allow anyone to tease, laugh, or imitate your child's speech mistakes. Privately, talk to her preschool teacher or babysitter and explain her difficulties with sounds. Offer some ideas to help when she has difficulty talking. If she has older siblings, talk to them and enlist their help in modeling good sound productions. When your child talks to a stranger, step into the role of translator if necessary. Of course, don't step in unless she is obviously frustrated and needs your help.

8. Do you expect your child to try to speak clearly?
    Yes ____ No ____

    Correct Answer: Yes. It's important for you to encourage and expect your child to try to speak the best she can. Be patient and also tell her how proud you are of her when she tries her best.

9. Do you prepare your child for new situations?
    Yes ____ No ____

    Correct Answer: Yes. Children who must struggle to communicate often feel self-conscious or apprehensive, especially when facing the unknown. Talk to your child about a new situation she may be facing. Rehearse the words she might hear or say in this situation. Ask your librarian to help you find a book about an upcoming situation, such as a trip to the hospital, the birth of a new sibling, or the first day at school.

TRAINING THE EAR: MODELING CORRECT SPEECH SOUNDS

To sharpen your child's ability to hear and make sounds, you must make individual sounds come alive. Being able to say a sound in isolation (e.g., the /b/ sound at the beginning of "boy" or the /s/ sound at the beginning of "sit") is often the first step in combining sounds into meaningful words. Over-enunciate the sounds for your child and encourage her to make the sounds and pretend with you. Remember, your child's pronunciation may not be perfect. However, giving her the chance to hear the sound many times will make it easier for her to say it when she is developmentally ready.

- Say "f . . . ." as you pretend you are an angry cat.

- Say "z . . . ." as you pretend you are a buzzing bee.

- Say "v . . . ." as you pretend you are a pesky mosquito.

- Say "s . . . . " as you pretend you are a slithering snake.

- Say "r . . . ." as you pretend you are an angry tiger.

- Say "g . . . . " as you pretend you are drinking a cup of water.

- Say "sh . . . . " as you pretend to put a dolly to sleep.

- Say "m . . . ." as you pretend to eat your favorite food.

- Sing "la, la, la" to the words of your favorite song.

- Move your arms like a clock and say "t-t-t."

Sound Activities

In the following sections, you will find sound activities for these sounds: /p/, /b/, /m/; /f/, /v/; /sh/, /ch/, /j/; /s/, /z/; /l/; /k/, /g/; /r/.

These activities are simple and fun ways to give your child many opportunities to hear a sound pronounced correctly in the initial, medial, and final positions of words. This will make it easier for her to hear the difference between the correct and incorrect productions of sounds, and make it easier to say the sound when she is developmentally ready. The following instructions refer to all the sound activities that follow. Please refer to them often.

INSTRUCTIONS

1. Most of the sound activities do not require any special props and can be done as you and your child go about your daily life activities: riding in the car, making dinner, or waiting in line. For a young child, learning is play, and these activities offer many ways to join in the fun rather than passively letting good teaching opportunities slip by.

2. The target word, the word that an activity emphasizes, is *italicized*. The target sound, the sound that the activity emphasizes, is underlined. When doing the activity, use these words as often as you can. Over-enunciate the underlined sound by saying it louder and longer. For example: In the /p/, /b/, and /m/ sound activities, you will find "Blow bubbles and say "pop!" While doing this activity with your child, you will use the words "blow," "bubbles," and "pop" as often as you can. You will over-emphasize (say the sound louder and longer) the /b/ sound in "blow," the /b/ sounds in "bubbles," and the /p/ sounds in "pop" whenever you say these words.

3. At times, encourage your child to watch your mouth as you make the sound. In addition to hearing how the sound is made, your child will also see how the sound is produced. For example, point to your lips when you make a /p/, /b/, or /m/ sound; point to your throat when you make a /g/ sound; point to your tongue when you make an /l/ sound.

4. If your child pronounces the target word correctly, praise her and help her hear the difference between the correct and incorrect productions. *Example:* "I like how you said 'house,' instead of 'hou.'"

5. If your child says the target word incorrectly, repeat the word correctly, saying the error sound louder and longer. Do not ask

her to repeat the word. Continue to use the word as often as you can as you continue the activity.

6. Tune into your child and follow her lead. Give her a chance to respond and express her own thoughts and ideas. Keep playing and talking as long as she is interested.

EXERCISE 13: P, B, and M Sound Activities

These activities will give your child many opportunities to hear the correct production of /p/, /b/, and /m/ in words. Remember, while doing the activities, use the italicized word as often as possible and over-emphasize the underlined sound in the word by saying it louder and longer. This instruction should be followed in all of the exercises below.

EXERCISES TO INCREASE LIP STRENGTH FOR PRODUCTION OF /b/, /p/, AND /m/

1. Blow bubbles.

2. Blow kisses. How many can you blow in eight seconds?

3. Blow whistles or party favors.

4. Blow on a pinwheel.

5. Hum your favorite song together.

Activities

/b/ Wave and say *bye-bye*.

Hit a *balloon* and talk about where the *balloon* lands.

Play with a *ball*.

Bake banana bread together.

Play "Guess what *number* I'm thinking of."

Give your child riddles. It is the *number* that tells your age? It is the *number* of sisters you have. And so on.

Find the longest, shortest, widest, and narrowest *tables* in your house.

Practice saying the *alphabet*.

Eat some corn on the *cob*.

Count the door *knobs* in your house.

Talk about a *job* that a familiar person has.

/p/ *Blow* *bubbles* and say "*pop!*"

Play with a *boat* and say "*putt-putt*."

Play with *puppets*.

Practice *hopping* and *skipping* around the yard.

Peel an *apple* and talk about how it looks and feels. Talk about apple foods: *apple juice, apple pie, apple cobbler, applesauce*.

Make a list of things that are made of *paper*.

Talk about words that are *opposites*: Ask, "What is the *opposite* of day?" Keep changing the word. *Examples:* "*boy*," "hot," "old," "*happy*," "sit," "run," "clean."

Talk about things that make you feel *happy*.

While driving in the car, count the *stop* signs you see.

/m/ Look at pictures of *mom*.

Look at the *mail* together or take a trip to the post office to see the *mail* carriers.

Talk about things to do with your *mouth*. *Examples:* eating, kissing, blowing, singing, *humming*.

Talk about why you do or do not need an *umbrella* today.

Take pictures with a *camera*.

Learn how to do a *somersault*.

Play a *game* together.

Talk about the lines on your *palm*.

Talk about creatures that are wild and those that are *tame*.

Word Lists: Use the following words to create your own sound activities for /b/, /p/, and /m/.

Initial Sounds: ball, bug, bus, boy, bear, boat, bowl, belt; pig, pants, pot, pepper, panda, paint, purse, puppy; man, money, mouse, mitten, mirror, music, moon

Medial Sounds: trouble, pebble, neighbor, rabbit; napkin, popcorn, pumpkin, purple; mermaid, amount, amen, America

Final Sounds: job, crab, crib, tube, comb; mop, hop, skip, lamp, wipe, cup; some, thumb, stem, him, name

Books to Read Aloud: While listening to you read the following books aloud, your child will have many opportunities to hear the /b/, /p/, and /m/ sounds pronounced correctly:

Goodnight Moon by Margaret Wise Brown (1991)

More, More, More, Said the Baby by Vera Williams (1997)

Hop on Pop by Dr. Seuss (1991)

A Bug, a Bear, and a Boy Go to School by David McPhail (1999)

EXERCISE 14: F and V Sound Activities

The following activities will give your child many opportunities to hear correct production of /f/ and /v/ sounds in words.

/**f**/ Make a *fan* out of paper and *fan* yourself.

Before bed, talk about all the *fun* you had today.

Say, "I had *fun* when we _____."

Play *football*.

Go *fishing* or talk about the *fish* you see behind the *fish* counter at the supermarket or at a pet store.

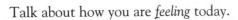

Talk about how you are *feeling* today.

Play, "Is it *food*?" Ask questions like, "Is an apple *food*?" "Is a couch *food*?"

Talk about things you can do with your *feet*.

Make a "*favorites*" list (*favorite* song, *food*, sport, animal).

Count the ways that you can move *forward* across the room (for example, jumping, hopping, running, walking, crawling, slithering, etc.).

Count to *five*: "one, two, three, *four*, *five*", or find *five* objects (doors, chairs, windows, etc.).

Ask your child to pretend she is an *elephant*, *goldfish*, or a *buffalo*. Talk about where you might *live* and what you would eat.

/**v**/ Talk about the places you would like to *visit*. Are they near or *far* away?

While driving, count the *vans* you see.

Play with cars and say "*vroom, vroom*."

Make a special *valentine* together.

Take a walk and look for *violets*. Pick some *flowers* and put them in a *vase*.

Talk about what you would do at a *carnival*.

Help your child plan a pretend *Thanksgiving feast* for her toys. Who would she *invite* and what *seven* kinds of *food* would she *serve*.

Count the *five fingers* on one hand and the *five* toes on one *foot*.

Talk about where insects and animals *live*. *Example:* Bears *live* in a *cave*. Bees *live* in a *hive*.

Word Lists: Use the following words to create your own sound activities for the /f/ and /v/ sounds.

Initial Sounds: farm, fast, family, father, far, fence, finger, five, fish, fix, fork, four; vase, very, visit, voice, veggies

Medial Sounds: traffic, before, after, rainfall, thankful, laughing; movie, ever, over, shovel, never, even

Final Sounds: laugh, puff, elf, sniff, knife, rough; move, love, stove, twelve, above, have, hive

Books to Read Aloud: While listening to you read the following books aloud, your child will have many opportunities to hear the /f/ and /v/ sounds pronounced correctly:

Don't Forget the Bacon by Pat Hutchings (1989)

Fix-It by David McPhail (2002)

Jack and the Beanstalk by Steven Kellogg (1997)

The Foot Book by Dr. Seuss (1996)

See the Fly Fly by Catherine Chase (1979)

EXERCISE 15: SH, CH, and J Sound Activities

The following activities will give your child many opportunities to hear the correct production of /sh/, /ch/, and /j/ sounds in words.

/**sh**/ Talk about different kinds of <u>sh</u>oes. Count the <u>sh</u>oes in your house.

Collect <u>sh</u>ells on the bea<u>ch</u>.

Talk about the <u>sh</u>apes you see as you ride in the car, or take a walk around the block.

Make <u>sh</u>amrock cookies.

On a sunny day, go outside and see your <u>sh</u>adow.

Find five things that you can <u>sh</u>ut.

Pu<u>sh</u> your child on swing and talk about other things you can pu<u>sh</u>.

Ma<u>sh</u> some potatoes for dinner.

Talk about what makes your child spe<u>ci</u>al.

/**ch**/ Play with a <u>ch</u>oo <u>ch</u>oo train.

<u>Ch</u>op vegetables.

Eat <u>ch</u>erries, <u>ch</u>icken, or <u>ch</u>eese.

Place a penny in one of your closed hands. Ask your child to find the penny by <u>ch</u>oosing the correct hand. Ask, "Which hand do you <u>ch</u>oose?"

Count the <u>ch</u>airs in your house. How many <u>ch</u>airs did you find?

Pretend you are in a parade and mar<u>ch</u> around the living room.

Talk about the two meanings for the word "pit<u>ch</u>er."

Eat your lun<u>ch</u> in a special place. What kind of sandwi<u>ch</u> are you eating?

Talk about things you can tou<u>ch</u> . . . cannot tou<u>ch</u> . . . and should never tou<u>ch</u>.

/j/ Count the *jars* in your *refrigerator*.

Practice *jumping* over items in your yard.

Talk about how *joy* means feeling happy. Talk about what makes you feel *joy*.

How many kinds of *jewelry* can you name?

Play "What if . . . ?" *Examples:* "What if you were a *giant*, what if you saw a *giraffe* in the yard, or what if you were a *teenager*."

Practice doing *jumping jacks*.

Word Lists: Use the following words to create your own sound activities for the /sh/, /ch/, and /j/ sounds.

Initial Sounds: share, shower, shoes, she, show, sharp, ship, should; chair, chicken, chin, cheeks, child, change, chalk; job, joke, jolly, jelly, jet, jacket, juice, just

Medial Sounds: sunshine, pushing, wishing, washing; catching, furniture, kitchen, marches, potato chip, teacher; blue jay, danger, engine, magic, soldier

Final Sounds: wish, wash, trash, crash, dish; beach, match, crunch, fetch, much, touch; bridge, large, age, cage, page, judge

Books to Read Aloud: While listening to you read the following books aloud, your child will have many opportunities to hear the /sh/, /ch/, and /j/ sounds pronounced correctly:

Peter's Chair by Ezra Jack Keats (1998)

Charlie and the Chocolate Factory by Roald Dahl (2002)

Carl Goes Shopping by Alexandra Day (1992)

Sheep in a Jeep by Nancy E. Shaw (1997)

Giraffes Can't Dance by Giles Andreae and Guy Parker-Rees (2001)

EXERCISE 16: S and Z Sound Activities

The following activities will give your child many opportunities to hear the correct production of /s/ and /z/ sounds in words.

/s/ Play *Simon Says*.

Listen to the *sounds* you hear in the kitchen, in the car, or in the backyard.

Let your child help you put *pairs* of *socks* together to make a match. Talk about how they are the *same* and how they are different.

Talk about what *makes* you feel *sad*.

Make a list of things that we can *sit* on.

Talk about how things *taste*. How many *salty* things can you name? How many *sour* things can you name? How many *sweet* things can you name?

Play on the *seesaw* at the park.

As you drive, talk about the *signs* you are *seeing*.

Describe an object and ask your child to *guess* what you are talking about.

Play a board game and talk about *tossing* the *dice* on each turn.

Make a *salad* together and talk about the *ingredients*. *Examples: cucumbers, tomatoes*. (These ending sounds are pronounced /z/.)

/z/ Visit the *zoo* and talk about the *animals* that the *zookeeper* takes care of.

Practice *zipping* your *zipper* all by *yourself*.

Talk about what "*zero*" means.

Plan a *surprise* for someone in your family.

Play "Which animal am I thinking of?" Ask, "Which animal *likes carrots* . . . *bananas* . . . *bones* . . . *acorns* . . . , and so forth?"

Draw a picture of three things: You might draw three *balls*, *cats*, *trees*, and so forth.

Practice walking on your *tiptoes*.

Put on some *music* and *dance* around the living room.

Let your child pick *dessert* for tonight's dinner.

Talk about things you can *smell* with your *nose*.

Make loud and *soft noises*. Talk about things that make *noise*.

Word Lists: Use the following words to create your own sound activities for the /s/ and /z/ sounds.

Initial Sounds: sun, sunshine, side, summer, sandwich, secret, seed, send, seven, sign, sidewalk, sing; zany, zap, zebra, zero, zip, zipper, zoo

Medial Sounds: sister, kissing, chasing, missing, ice cream, glasses, beside, listen, baseball, himself, herself; busy, scissors, tossing, buzzing, oozing, snoozing, using, zigzag

Final Sounds: Fence, toss, kiss, face, mice, mouse, loose, lettuce, juice, dress, chase; cheese, nose, his, was, is, buzz, fuzz, does, was, has

Words that mean "more than one" may have either an /s/ or a /z/ sound at the end. *Examples:* houses, bikes, monkeys, toys, and so on.

Books to Read Aloud: While listening to you read the following books aloud, your child will have many opportunities to hear the /s/ and /z/ sounds pronounced correctly.

Berlioz the Bear by Jan Brett (1996)

A Zoo for Mister Muster by Arnold Lobel (1962)

Zella, Zack and Zodiac by Bill Peet (1989)

Bob's Busy Saw by Kiki Thorpe (2002)

The Snowy Day by Ezra Jack Keats (1962)

EXERCISE 17: L Sound Activities

The following activities will give your child many opportunities to hear the correct production of the /l/ sound in words.

/l/ _Lick_ a _lollipop._

Find colorful _leaves_ in the _fall._

Visit a _library_ and read one of the books mentioned below.

Play _Follow the Leader._

Talk about _left_ and right. Give your child directions to _follow._

Give your child directions to _line_ up her toys. "Put the bear _last._"

Count the _lamps_ in your _living_ room.

Make _lemonade_ together. Talk about how many _lemons_ you are using.

Make a _necklace_ out of pasta pieces or beads.

Make a _list_ of things you _love_ to do or people you _love._

Talk about a _lifeguard's_ job. Talk about why you would or why you would not _like_ to be a _lifeguard._

Word Lists: Use the following words to create your own sound activities for the /l/ sound.

Initial Sounds: lion, lock, lamb, lady, lake, lemon, Lucy, land, less, ladder, large, listen, lobster, loud, low, leg, leopard

Medial Sounds: along, always, balloon, color, dollar, gallop, melting, pillow, polite, sailing, swallow, falling, telling, willow

Final Sounds: ball, bottle, dull, fall, fell, mall, mile, pole, school, seal, sell, snail, tall, wall, well

Books to Read Aloud: While listening to you read the following books aloud, your child will have many opportunities to hear the /l/ sound pronounced correctly:

Larabee by Kevin Luthardt (2004)

The Happy Lion by Louise Fatio (2004)

Don't Get Lost by Pat Hutchins (2004)

Lizard Walinsky by Robert Baker (2004)

EXERCISE 18: K and G Sound Activities

The following activities will give your child many opportunities to hear the correct production of the /k/ and /g/ sounds in words.

/**k**/ Play with <u>c</u>ars in a toy <u>g</u>ara<u>g</u>e.

Look for <u>c</u>ats in your neighborhood or <u>c</u>ats in pictures.

Bake a <u>c</u>a<u>k</u>e, <u>c</u>oo<u>k</u>ies, or <u>c</u>up<u>c</u>a<u>k</u>es with your child.

Hop around the yard like a <u>k</u>angaroo.

<u>C</u>olor a <u>c</u>ard for someone who is having a special day.

<u>K</u>i<u>ck</u> a ball.

Talk about the <u>k</u>eys on your <u>k</u>ey chain. What is each <u>k</u>ey used for?

Talk about how we tal<u>k</u>. (See chapter 3.)

Pretend it is April Fool's Day and play a jo<u>k</u>e on someone.

What does win<u>k</u> mean? Can you win<u>k</u>?

Blin<u>k</u> your eyes.

/g/ Give your child directions to stop and *go* as she performs a specified action.

Talk about what you might plant in a *garden*.

Talk about a *gift* for Dad, Brother, <u>G</u>*randmother*, or a friend.

Use social *greetings* often. *Examples: good-bye, good morning, good night.*

Crack an *egg* and talk about what you see inside. Talk about the parts of an *egg* (yolk, *eggshell*).

Word Lists: Use the following words to create your own sound activities for the /g/ and /k/ sounds.

Initial Sounds: go, good, game, garden, get, give, gate, girl, gave, gum, golf; cake, can, candy, car, cap, class, coat, cold, comb, count, crow, cuddle

Medial Sounds: again, dragon, eggshell, seagull, sugar, jogging, wagon, finger; ankle, blanket, cookie, cocoa, include, anchor

Final Sounds: beg, big, bug, dig, dog, egg, frog, hog, hug, leg; bike, check, clock, dark, deck, desk, drink, duck, lake, sock, skunk, take, trick, truck, trunk

Books to Read Aloud: While listening to you read the following books aloud, your child will have many opportunities to hear the /g/ and /k/ sounds pronounced correctly:

A Girl, a Goat, and a Goose by David McPhail (2000)

Cows in the Kitchen by June Crebbin (2003)

How Many Kisses Do You Want Tonight? by Varsha Bajaj (2004)

Goosie by Olivier Dunrea (2002)

EXERCISE 19: R Sound Activities

The following activities will give your child many opportunities to hear the correct production of the /r/ sound in words.

/r/ Before bed, talk about *tomorrow*. What day will *tomorrow* be? What will you do *tomorrow*?

Play a game and say "my *turn*" each time it is your chance to play.

Play "things that go *together*." Ask your child, "What goes with shoes . . . table . . . *chair* . . . hat . . . coat . . . etc." Repeat her answer by saying, "Yes, shoes and socks go *together*."

Draw a *rainbow*.

Talk about things that are *red*, *round*, and *rough*.

Talk about things you can *ride*.

Count the *rooms* in your house.

Put objects in a *row*.

Sing "*Row*, *Row*, *Row* *Your* Boat" together.

Talk about what kind of *cereal* you would like for *breakfast*.

Talk about what *third* means.

Word Lists: Use the following words to create your own sound activities for the /r/ sound.

Initial Sounds: rainbow, rain, red, rest, ribbon, right, ring, river, road, rock, roll, roof, room, run, rose

Medial Sounds: airplane, berry, bird, birthday, carrot, chirp, fairy, girl, person, squirrel, work

Final Sounds: butter, car, chair, chore, door, father, fire, four, her, hurt, purr, stir, thunder, washer, year, your

Use comparative words. *Examples:* colder, hotter, older, younger, smaller, bigger

Books to Read Aloud: While listening to you read the following books aloud, your child will have many opportunities to hear the /r/ sounds pronounced correctly:

Little Rabbit Goes to School by Harry Horse (2004)

The Little Blue Rabbit by Angela McAllister (2003)

The Kissing Hand by Audrey Penn (1993)

Fire Truck by Peter Sis (1998)

Roller Coaster by Marla Frazee (2003)

PRETEND PLAY

You may recall a fond memory from childhood of sitting at small table and pretending to have a tea party with your mom or dad. Or perhaps you remember playing inside of the enormous cardboard box that once held your family's new refrigerator. As the box became your own special place for pretend games, the possibilities were endless. Pretend play is usually accompanied by plenty of words and actions. Your child not only needs to hear sounds said correctly many times, she also needs a lot of practice listening to herself saying sounds.

By accepting and encouraging your child to spend time in the world of make-believe, you enhance her self-awareness, self-control, and self-confidence, and you give her many opportunities to practice saying speech sounds and expressing herself. Pretend play has a positive influence on a child's memory and language skills, too (Hughes, Noppe, and Noppe 1996).

Infants

Pretend play with your child can begin shortly after birth. Begin early and encourage your child to pretend by pretending with her. Encourage her to copy your tongue movements, gestures, or sounds. Sing songs and let her dance in your arms..

Two- to Three Years Old

Two- and three-years-olds often like to live out their fantasies and explore their emotions by talking to themselves and using the words they know. You may have heard your child pretend that she is someone else as she falls asleep, plays in the bathtub, or rides in the car.

Offer encouragement and suggestions. When you see or hear your child engaged in pretend play, offer encouragement and suggestions. If she seems stuck, elaborate on what she is doing or suggest a new direction. *Examples:* If she's pretending to give her teddy bear a bath, suggest that she wash his hair next. If she's pushing a truck across the floor, ask her what kind of ice cream she's selling today, or offer her pretend barking dog a pretend bone.

PROPS FOR PRETENDING

- Generally, children at this age have an interest in doing household chores. Under close supervision, provide lots of toys or safe real objects that you use around your home. Pans, wooden spoons, lids, plastic cups, or kitchen utensils are great.

- Many children also enjoy pretending to be other people, such as cowboys, firefighters, or nurses. Because changing clothing for a costume is too hard for such a young child, fill a box with some simple props for pretending, such as an old purse, ties, scarves, adult-size gloves, a nightgown, and different hats for pretending.

■ Your child may love to create situations with miniature toys, such as animals or cars. Toy vehicles are often favorites at this age because they can be used for fantasy and action play. When your child pretends that a cardboard box is a car, pushing it across the floor and saying, "vroom vroom," she is learning symbols—how one thing can stand for another. In later years, this knowledge may be a key factor in learning letters and numbers as symbols.

■ Real-world experiences will also encourage your child to dream and pretend. Playing with her dump truck may take on a whole new meaning after observing a real construction site in action.

Four to Six Years Old

Between four years and six years of age, your child will enjoy many aspects of imaginary and dramatic play. You'll be amazed as she acts out her understanding of the world and its people, and not just those that are part of her life. As she pretends, you may hear her asking and answering questions that go with her actions. You may observe her acting out an upcoming doctor's appointment or an overnight stay at Grandmother's house.

For encouraging pretend play, the following suggestions may prove useful:

■ Gather small props, including an overnight bag, an apron, scarves, hats, or any old clothes you have around the house. Put them in an easily accessible box.

■ Don't throw away your old greeting cards, paper tubing from paper towel or aluminum foil rolls, shirt cardboard, or gift wrap. These make great pretend props, too. Gift, shoe, jewelry, oatmeal, spaghetti, or small appliance boxes can also stimulate a young child's imagination. Watch as they transmute into building blocks, musical instruments, or storage space for collecting treasures.

■ Provide places for imaginary play, such as tents, a sandbox, a swing set, or a climbing gym. If you don't have a tent, a blanket thrown over four straight-backed chairs makes a wonderful "cave."

■ Give your child a small white sheet. Watch her transform herself into a ghost, snowwoman, or superhero. She may use it as a cover for napping or as a blanket for a picnic in the living room. Drape it over two chairs and make a fort. Bring a flashlight inside and read a book together.

■ Spark her imagination with creative materials, such as clay, finger paints, or scented markers.

■ Go on a nature hike together and fill a paper bag with interesting treasures. Encourage her to use the leaves, pinecones, or twigs she collects to create collages of her own.

■ While waiting in line or riding in the car, use the power of words to foster your child's imagination. Play "What if" by asking her open-ended questions, like "If you were a giant, what would you do?" or "What would happen if you lived in the zoo?"

7 Developing Phonological Awareness

Usually, parents are more concerned about their child's ability to read than they are about any other skill taught in school. This makes sense because reading is essential for understanding and gaining knowledge about the world all through life. More than two decades of research have shown that phonological awareness is an important skill that sets the foundation for the development of literacy. *Phonological awareness* refers to the awareness of words, syllables, or phonemes, and the ability to notice, think about, or manipulate the sounds in language (Torgesen, Wagner, and Rashotte 1997). It involves learning about the structure of words rather than their meaning.

Children who become successful readers have strong phonological awareness skills long before they begin formal reading instruction. Children with poor phonological awareness skills have greater difficulty learning to read (Stackhouse 1997). In fact, numerous studies have shown that phonological awareness is a better predictor of how well a child will learn to read than reading readiness, listening-comprehension tests, or a child's general intelligence (Stanovich 1996).

The activities to build phonological awareness outlined in Exercise 19 below would benefit all children, but especially children who may have speech and language problems. There is strong evidence that children who have significant difficulty learning how to say speech sounds correctly do not perform well on phonological awareness tasks (Hodson 1998), and are more likely to struggle with literacy acquisition than children with normal speech development (Nathan et al. 2004). Raising your own awareness of the importance of phonological awareness may encourage you to do these activities with your child frequently.

HOW DOES SPOKEN LANGUAGE WORK?

To be able to read and understand spoken language, your child must develop a strong understanding of how the words in our language are represented in print. First, sentences can be divided into words and words can be divided into syllables. For example, "bat" has one syllable, "bat"; sunshine has two syllables, "sun" and "shine." These syllables are made up of the smallest units of sound, called *phonemes*.

A word is made up of strings of phonemes. For example, "hat" has three phonemes (sounds): /h/, /a/, and /t/. Your child develops phonological awareness when he can hear the phonemes that make up words and understand how these sound segments can be taken apart, put back together, and rhymed. When a child becomes aware of phonemes (the individual sounds in words), it makes learning phonics (letters and the sounds they make) easier, and it fosters the child's understanding of how words are represented in print (Christensen 1997). Children are then able to understand why they learn the individual sounds of letters, and, as a result, "sounding out" words in beginning reading makes more sense to them (Liberman, Shankweiler, and Liberman 1989).

Important Skills to Learn

Phonological awareness involves mastering the skills listed below:

- **Awareness of sounds.** Your child must be able to recognize and hear the difference between the sounds he hears

(Friel-Patti 1998). Children must also be able to remember the order in which the sounds and words they hear were presented.

■ **Rhyming.** Begin early and give your child many experiences with nursery rhymes. Several researchers have concluded that children who are familiar with nursery rhymes at age three tend to be more highly developed in general phonological awareness by age four, and in phonemic awareness by age six (Bryant et al. 1990). (*Phonemic awareness* refers to awareness of the individual sounds in words—phonemes. *Phonological awareness* generally refers to the awareness of words, syllables, and phonemes.) When children hear a lot of rhymes and learn to rhyme words themselves, it gives them insight into the sounds in words, rather than just what the words mean. They learn how to focus on parts of a word, rather than how it sounds as a whole. This helps them understand that many different words share common sounds and common letter sequences. This understanding makes a significant contribution to developing strategies for reading words (Bryant 1990).

■ **Sound blending.** Sound blending is the ability to take isolated syllables or sounds and combine them together into a sequence that produces a recognizable world. For example; say "/t/, /o/, /p/" slowly. When you blend these sounds together, you say the word "top." This important skill is needed when a child is learning to decode or sound out printed words phonetically.

■ **Sound segmentation.** Segmenting sounds is the skill that shows a child how to identify individual syllables and sounds within words and break them apart. For example, if you were segmenting the word "put," you would say: "/p/, /u/, /t/." Experts believe that when children realize that speech can be segmented into units represented by letters, that helps them grasp how letters represent sounds for reading and writing tasks.

- **Sound manipulation.** This is the ability to change a word by deleting, adding, or substituting the sounds in the word. For example, /b/, /a/, /t/ says "bat." If you delete the /b/ sound, it says "at." If you substitute a /c/ for the /b/ sound, it says "cat."

HOW PARENTS CAN HELP

Most children who develop strong phonological awareness before they begin formal reading instruction become successful readers. The National Association of School Psychologists recommends that parents begin to train phonological awareness skills by using adult-directed instructions with developmentally appropriate activities (National Association of School Psychologists 2002).

The exercises below are presented in the order in which the skills are usually developed by children (Ehri et al. 2001). Some children may learn several skills at once. These are all oral language tasks and do not require your child to have any knowledge of the alphabet. While doing the exercises, remember to say the sound the letter makes, rather than the letter name. For example, when using the sound /b/, you would not say "bee," like the insect, but rather the sound the letter b makes or "buh." Also, remember to be sensitive to the sounds your child may have difficulty saying. Many young children cannot say all the sounds of their language correctly until they are seven or older.

In these exercises, your child may need several examples before he can do the specified task independently. In addition, to master a skill, most children will need a lot of repetition and practice. Give your child positive feedback by praising a correct answer or by letting him know that you appreciate how hard he is trying, even when the answer is incorrect. If he doesn't answer correctly, explain the correct answer and give him several more examples before asking him to answer independently again. You might try using different words or pictures to illustrate your example, or you could try the trouble-shooting activity. Many of these activities provide additional visual clues to help your child understand the concept presented.

These exercises and examples are only a starting point. The resources provided will give you many more activities to reinforce these skills. **Note:** It is very important to create a mood of playfulness and fun, rather than drill and repetition, to ensure that you and your child both enjoy the time spent together.

EXERCISE 20: Twenty-five Activities to Improve Your Child's Phonological Awareness

1. **Skill: Hearing how sounds are the same and how they are different.** Give your child many opportunities to hear sounds by calling attention to the sounds in your natural environment. Use these words to describe and compare the sounds you hear: "loud," "quiet," "high," "low," "same," and "different."

    Sample activity: Talk about the sounds that different animals make. Are they loud or soft sounds? Sing "Old McDonald Had a Farm."

2. **Skill: Locating the source of a sound you hear.** Give your child many opportunities to sharpen his ability to focus on the sound he hears, and to isolate one sound from the background of the other sounds he hears. This is important because your young child must learn how to focus on what the teacher says, even when there is activity and noise happening all around him. Knowing how to pay attention to the source of a sound will sharpen his ability to listen effectively.

    Sample activities: Hide a ticking clock and ask your child to find it. Take a "listening walk" around your neighborhood and listen for sounds. Talk about where the sounds come from.

3. **Skill: Remembering what you hear.** To learn to read, children must remember the sounds they hear and the order in which they were presented. Ask your child to repeat a word after you. Start with one-syllable words and then try longer words. Vary the vowel and consonant combinations.

Sample Activity

Adult: Say the word after I say it. Ready? Hat.

Child: Hat.

Adult: Nice job. Let's do it again. Ready? Hut.

Child: Hut.

Adult: Good.

Sample words: pay, paint, eel, ill, ache, stew, mile, meal, sly, tear

Next, give your child longer words to repeat after you.

Adult: Say the word after I say it. Ready? Baby.

Child: Baby.

Adult: Good listening.

4.   **Skill: Developing awareness of words.** While reading a book or looking at signs, talk about long words and short words. *Examples:* long words such as "celebrate" and "animal," and short words such as "hat," "stop," and "yield." Count the letters in a word or the words on a page.

Sample Activity

Adult: This word says "hat." Let's count the letters together.

Adult and
Child: One ... two ... three ...

Adult: Yes, "hat" has three letters. It is a short word.

5.   **Skill: Hearing the difference between the words you expect to hear and the words you actually do hear.** Without prior explanation, while reading a story, singing a song, reciting rhymes, or giving your child a simple direction, replace a familiar word with a nonsense word. Encourage your child to listen closely to hear the word that you substituted incorrectly. See if he can tell you what you meant to say.

Sample Activity

Adult: Let's go to the post office to buy a loaf of bread.

Child: What? Did you mean let's go to the store?

Adult: Oh yes, good listening. Let's go to the store to buy a loaf of bread, not to the post office.

Troubleshooting: Practice this skill in a structured activity. First explain that you are going to say a silly sentence. Then ask your child to tell you what word doesn't make sense and which word would make sense. Use a familiar context for your child. *Example:* "We have a great big lion as our pet."

6. **Skill:** Separating sentences into words. Say a sentence and pause between the words. Ask your child to clap each time he hears a different word.

Sample Activity

Adult: I'm going to say a sentence slowly and I'm going to stop for a while between each word. Listen, "I . . . am . . . happy." How many words did you hear in that sentence?

Child: Three!

Adult: Yes, "I" is one, "am" is two, and "happy" is three. Next, try clapping every time you hear me say a different word and we will count the claps. Ready? "I . . . am . . . happy . . . today."

Child: Claps four times.

Adult: Yes, there are four words in that sentence.

Troubleshooting: Give your child a collection of objects, such as pennies or dry pasta pieces. Instruct him to move one forward every time he hears a word. When you finish saying the sentence, count the objects to see how many words were in the sentence.

7. **Skill: Learning about words that rhyme.** Recite nursery rhymes and poems often to your young child. As you recite, whisper the rhyming words or say them louder than the other words. Also, practice listening to rhymes in songs.

   Books that contain rhymes: *Chicka Chicka Boom Boom*, by Bill Martin and John Archambault, 2000; *Read-Aloud Rhymes for the Very Young*, by Jack Prelutsky, 1986; *The Cat in the Hat Comes Back*, by Dr. Seuss, 1958; *One Odd Old Owl*, by Paul Adshead, 1996; and *Each Peach Pear Plum*, by Janet and Allan Ahlberg, 1999.

   Song Resources

   Books: *Phonemic Awareness Songs & Rhymes* (Grades Pre-K to 2), by Wiley Blevins, 2004; *Build Early Literacy Skills*, by Jean Feldman, 2002.

   Audio CDs: *Bahama Pajamas*, by Joe Scruggs, 1990; *Can a Cherry Pie Wave Goodbye?* by Hap Palmer, 2002; *Can Cookatoos Count by Twos?* by Hap Palmer, 2002; *I'm All Ears: Sing into Reading*, by Fran Avni, 1999; *Alpha Songs*, by Greg Whitfield, 1997.

8. **Skill: Rhyming during daily life activities.** Talk about words that rhyme with things that you and your child are seeing and doing.

   Sample activities: While cooking dinner, talk about how "cook" rhymes with "look" and "book." "Dishes" rhymes with "fishes" and "wishes." Make up silly or nonsensical rhymes too. For example, use words that rhyme with your child's name or with an object you are using.

9. **Skill: Fill in the missing word or phrase that rhymes.** Sing part of a familiar song or recite a nursery rhyme and have your child fill in the missing word that rhymes. When he is able to do this, try singing part of a familiar song or reciting a nursery rhyme and encourage him to supply the missing phrase. First help him repeat the familiar and repetitive phrases by saying

them together. Next, sing or recite only part of the song or rhyme and see whether he can supply the missing phrase.

Sample Activity

Adult: Humpty Dumpty sat on a wall. Humpty Dumpty had a great _____.

Child: Fall!

Adult: That's right.

10. **Skill: Saying familiar rhymes independently.** Say a familiar rhyme. Stop before the end and ask your child to supply the missing words.

Sample Activity

Adult: Humpty Dumpty_____ . Can you finish the rhyme?

Child: Sat on a wall!

Adult: Great, can you tell me more? Humpty

_____ .

Child: Dumpty had a great fall?

Adult: Yes, he sat on the wall and had a great fall.

11. **Skill: Recognizing words that rhyme.** Give your child two words and see if he can tell you whether they rhyme. Next give him three words: two that rhyme, and one that doesn't. Ask him to tell you which word doesn't rhyme with the others.

Sample Activities

Adult: Let's talk about words that rhyme. "Man," "fan," and "pan" rhyme. Listen, touch your nose if you hear two words that rhyme. Ready? "Hat," "bat."

Child: Touches his nose.

Adult: Good listening. Yes, "hat," and "bat" rhyme.

> *Adult:*   Now, I'm going to say three words. Two of these words rhyme, one doesn't. Can you tell me which word doesn't rhyme with the others? Ready? "Sun," "boy," "fun."
>
> *Child:*   "Boy!"
>
> *Adult:*   Yes, "boy" doesn't rhyme with "sun" or "fun." It has a different sound at the end.

Troubleshooting: Use objects or pictures to represent the words. For example, show your child pictures of a man, a dog, and a pan. Say the words slowly as you point to the pictures. Ask him to point to the one that doesn't rhyme

12. **Skill: Say a word that rhymes with a target word.** Say a word and then ask your child to tell you a word that rhymes with that word. Even if he gives you an unrecognizable or a nonsense word that rhymes, accept it and praise him for giving you a correct answer. The purpose of this activity is to say a word that has the same ending sound, even if it isn't a real word.

Sample Activity

> *Adult:*   Can you tell me a word that rhymes with "head"?
>
> *Child:*   "Kead"?
>
> *Adult:*   Yes, "head" and "kead" rhyme.

Sample words to rhyme: boy, sun, fly, cow, pat, bed, pet, door, knee, bug, toe, boat

13. **Skill: Blend syllables into words.** Say a word slowly and pause between the syllables. Ask your child to say the word fast, putting the parts together to make a word that sounds real. Compound words (words that can be separated into two common words) are the easiest to blend and should be used in this activity.

Sample Activity

Adult: I'm going to say a word slowly and stop between each part. Then I'm going to say it faster and put the parts together. Listen, "hot . . . dog." When I say the word fast, it's "hot dog."

Adult: You try it. What word am I saying? "Cow . . . boy."

Child: "Cowboy."

Adult: Yes, "cow . . . boy" says "cowboy."

Sample words: baseball, houseboat, sunshine, playmate, schoolyard, sidewalk

Troubleshooting: Use a puppet to tell your child a familiar story. Have the puppet mispronounce a word by segmenting it into syllables. Ask your child to help the puppet put the word together again, so it can continue the story.

14. **Skill: Blend syllables into words using onset-rime words.** *Onset* means the beginning sound(s) or the sound before the first vowel. For example, in "cake" the onset is /c/. The first vowel and the rest of the word is called *rime* (Bowey and Francis 1991). The rime in "cake" is /ake/. Say a word slowly and pause between the onset and the rime of the word. Ask your child to blend the parts together to make a word that sounds real.

Sample Activity

Adult: I'm going to say a word slowly and stop between each part. Then I'm going to put the parts together. Listen, "fl . . . oor." When I say the word fast, it's "floor." Now, you try it. "Tr . . . uck."

Child: "Truck."

Adult: Yes, "tr . . . uck" says "truck."

Troubleshooting: If your child has difficulty with this task, show him a picture or point to the object you are naming.

Sample words: mash, beat, make, poke, band, bone, lake, vase, same, feel, chin, seat

15. **Skill: Recognizing words that start with the same sound.** Explain to your child that you are going to say a word and you want him to listen closely to the first sound of that word. Say a word, over-enunciating the beginning sound by repeating it several times before you say the whole word. Next, explain that you will say two more words: one will begin with the same sound as the first word, and the other will begin with a different sound. Ask your child to tell you which word has the same beginning sound as _____ (the first word should be repeated).

Sample Activity

Adult: Which word begins with the same sound as "/s/ ... /s/ ... /s/ ... sit"? "Side" or "mat"?

Child: "Side."

Adult: Yes, "side" and "sit" both begin with /s/.

Resources for Repeating the Initial Sound in Two or More Words (Alliteration)

Phonemic awareness: *Playing with Sound to Strengthen Beginning Reading Skills*, by Jo Fitzpatrick, 1997; *Animalia*, by Graeme Base, 1997; *The Accidental Zucchini: An Unexpected Alphabet*, by Max Grover, 1997; *Where Is Everybody? An Unexpected Alphabet*, by Eve Merriam, 1992.

16. **Skill: Saying words that start with the same sound.** Say a word, over-enunciating the beginning sound by repeating the sound several times before saying the whole word. Ask your child to think of a word that begins with the same sound.

Sample Activity

Adult: Can you think of a word that begins like "/t/ ... /t/ ... /t/ ... Tom"? (Emphasize the beginning sound by repeating it louder and holding it longer.)

Child: "Toy."

Adult: Yes. Listen, "Tom" and "toy" begin with the /t/ sound. The first sound is the same in both words.

Troubleshooting: Use pictures and objects to represent the words.

17. **Skill: Recognizing words that end with the same sound.** Explain to your child that you are going to say a word and that you want him to listen closely to the last sound of that word. Say a word, over-enunciating the ending sound by repeating it several times. Next, explain that you will say two more words and one will end with the same sound as the first word and the other will end with a different sound. Ask your child to tell you which word has the same ending sound as _____ (the first word should be repeated).

Sample Activity

Adult: Which word ends with the same sound as "pat . . . /t/ . . . /t/"? "Hat" or "run"?

Child: "Hat."

Adult: Yes, "pat" and "hat" both end with /t/.

18. **Skill: Saying words that end with the same sound.** Say a word, over-enunciating the ending sound by repeating the sound several times. Ask your child to think of a word that ends with the same sound.

Sample Activity

Adult: Can you think of a word that ends like "Nick . . . /k/ . . . /k/"? (Emphasize the ending sound by saying it louder and holding it longer.)

Child: "Pick."

Adult: Yes. Listen, "Nick" and "pick" both end with the /k/ sound. The ending sound is the same in both words.

Troubleshooting: Use pictures and objects to represent the words. Write the words under the pictures and point to the letters that look the same as you say them.

19. **Skill: Recognizing words that have the same medial sound.** Explain to your child that you are going to say a word and you want him to listen closely to the sound in the middle of that word. Say a word, over-enunciating the medial sound. Next, explain that you will say two more words and one will have the same sound in the middle as the first word and the other will have a different sound in the middle. Ask your child to tell you which work has the same sound in the middle as _____ (the first word should be repeated).

   Sample Activity

   Adult: Which word has the same sound in the middle as "apple"? "Monkey" or "mopping"?

   Child: "Mopping."

   Adult: Yes, "apple" and "mopping" both have the /p/ sound in the middle.

20. **Skill: Saying words that have the same medial sounds.** Say a word, over-enunciating the medial sound. Ask your child to think of a word that has the same sound in the middle.

   Sample Activity

   Adult: Can you think of a word that has the same sound in the middle as "monkey"?

   Child: "Looking"?

   Adult: Yes. Listen, "monkey" and "looking" both have the /k/ sound in the middle.

   Troubleshooting: Write the words and point out how the letters in the middle of the words look the same.

21. **Skill: Break words into individual sounds.** Say a word and ask
your child to repeat the word slowly, pausing between each
sound or part of the word. Begin with words that have two
sounds and then introduce longer words.

Sample Activity

Adult: I'm going to say a word. Next, I'll repeat the word
            and I'll say all the parts slowly. Listen, "/g/ . . .
            /o/." Now, you say the next word slowly so I can
            hear all the parts. Ready? "Go."

Child: "/g/ . . . /o/"

Adult: Yes, the parts of "go" are "/g/ . . . /o/."

Sample words for two sounds: toe, so, day, me, tie, row, do,
moo, shoe, who, chew, boo

Sample words for three sounds: ham, chill, beach, moon, wait,
teeth, rose, soak, hear, mine

22. **Skill: Sound manipulation—deleting sounds.** Say a word and
ask your child to say the word without the first sound.

Sample Activity

Adult: What word would be left if the /k/ was taken
            away from "cake"?

Child: "ake"?

Adult: Yes, "cake" without the /k/ sound is "ake."

Troubleshooting: If your child finds this concept difficult, try
this next activity first. Put four or five objects on the table.
Name each one and ask him to repeat the names of each after
you. Ask him to close his eyes as you remove one or two of the
objects. When he opens his eyes, ask him to tell you which
objects are missing from the table.

Sample words: /p/ taken away from "pit" (it); /k/ from "click"
(lick); /b/ from "break" (rake); /s/ from "smile" (mile)

23. **Skill: Blend three to four sounds into words.** Say a word that has three sounds, for example, "hat," and pause between the sounds: /h/ . . . /a/ . . . /t/. Ask your child to put the sounds together to make a word that sounds real. After your child can blend three sounds together, say words that have four sounds and ask him to blend the sounds together to make a real-sounding word.

Sample Activity

Adult: I'm going to say sounds that make up a word that you know. I'll say them slowly. Listen, /b/ . . . /a/ . . . /t/. (Say each sound slowly and pause between the sounds.) When I put these sounds together, /b/ /a/ /t/ says "bat." Now, listen to me say the words slowly and see if you can put them together. Ready? /m/ . . . /o/ . . . /p/.

Child: "Mop."

Adult: Yes, /m/ . . . /o/ . . . /p/ says "mop."

Troubleshooting: Visual clues, such as pictures or objects, may be helpful. Also, use categories, such as kinds of food, vehicles, or familiar names. Begin by explaining that the answers will be the name of a _____ .

Sample words for three sounds: hat, boot, back, sun, Tom, run, home, nose, toad, soap, rain, robe

Sample words for four sounds: smile, plate, steak, sand, flake, place, snail, paint, speak, stone

24. **Skill: Sound manipulation—adding sounds.** Say a word. Ask your child to take away the first sound and add another sound, and then to say the new word.

Sample Activity

Adult: What new word is made when you add /b/ to /at/?

Child: "Bat."

Adult: Yes, /b/ added to "at" says "bat."

Troubleshooting: If your child has trouble with this skill, put four or five objects on the table. Name each one and ask him to repeat the names after you. This time, when his eyes are closed, place an additional object on the table. Ask him to tell you which object was added to the table.

Sample words: add /b/ to "ring" (bring); add /f/ to "rose" (froze); add /d/ to "rink" (drink); add /s/ to "tick" (stick)

25. **Skill: Changing a sound in a word to make a new word.** Say a word and ask your child to change the initial sound to a different sound.

Sample Activity

Adult: Can you change the /c/ in "cat" to /m/? What new word did you make?

Child: "Mat."

Adult: Yes, if you change the /c/ in "cat" to /m/, it says "mat."

Troubleshooting: If your child is having difficulty with this skill, put four or five objects on the table. Name each one and ask your child to repeat the names after you. This time, when your child's eyes are closed, take away an object and substitute another one. Ask your child to tell you which object was taken away and which object has replaced it.

Sample words: Change the /h/ in "hot" to /p/ (pot); change the /k/ in "cake" to /m/ (make); change the /b/ in "bow" to /t/ (tow); change the /s/ in "sun" to /f/ (fun).

Your child's early literacy experiences will open the door to later academic performance. Start early and give him the knowledge and skills to stimulate his further growth and refinement of phonological awareness.

8 How to Find Professional Help

If you have concerns about your child's development in any area, it is always wise to seek professional help. Of course, you want this professional to be well educated, have experience with your child's type of difficulty, and be able to work well with her. This chapter focuses on how to find the right speech/language pathologist, and how to prepare yourself and your child for your first appointment.

Educating yourself about a speech and language evaluation may help you to feel more at ease, and that, in turn, will help your child feel more relaxed too. This may enable the speech/language pathologist to get an accurate picture of her ability to communicate. Moreover, knowing what to expect and how to prepare for the evaluation and therapy may help you gain more insight into your child's difficulties.

WHO CAN HELP YOUR CHILD?

A speech/language pathologist is trained to assess, treat, and help prevent speech, language, and voice problems in children (beginning at birth) and adults. These professionals are called "speech/language pathologists," "speech/language therapists" or "speech/language specialists." A professional will assess your child's communication strengths and weaknesses and, if necessary, will plan and carry out therapy to correct or modify the communication difficulty. A speech/language pathologist is often part of a health care or educational team depending on the nature of the problem. He or she may work closely with your child's physician, orthodontist, psychologist, educators, or social workers.

Where Can You Find a Speech/Language Pathologist?

A speech/language pathologist is trained to work in a variety of settings. These include:

- speech and hearing clinics that may be located in your local community

- colleges or universities

- hospitals or medical clinics

- local public schools

- private offices

You might ask your pediatrician to recommend a speech professional in your area, or you could ask a family member or friend for a referral. To find a speech/language pathologist close to your home, you can call your local school district, look in the yellow pages, or call the American Speech-Language-Hearing Association (1-800-638-8255). This organization (ASHA) is the professional, scientific, and credentialing association for audiologists, speech/language pathologists, and speech, language, and hearing scientists. Also, you can go the ASHA Web site (www.asha.org/default.htm) and click on "Find a Professional."

EXERCISE 21: Finding a Highly Qualified Therapist

Of course, you are interested in finding a therapist who is well educated, experienced, and will work well with your child. Here are some sample questions to ask the therapist before you make the first visit. He or she should be able to answer yes to all of the questions below:

1. Do you have a master's (or higher) degree?
    Yes _____ No _____

    A speech/language pathologist should have a master's or a doctorate. Usually, the bachelor's degree provides only an introduction to the theories of communication disorders and treatment. The master's degree gives the student more in-depth knowledge and practical experiences because students are supervised while they work with individuals who have various communication problems in a variety of settings.

2. Do you have any special certifications?
    Yes _____ No _____

    It's best to find a therapist who has received his or her certificate of clinical competence (CCC) from ASHA. You will see those initials after his or her name and degree, for example, Kimberly King, MS, CCC-SLP. These initials indicate that Ms. King has a master of science degree and that she has received her certificate of clinical competence in speech/language pathology from ASHA. All professionals who have a certificate of clinical competence have completed the following course work:

    - 27 semester credit hours in basic science.

    - 36 semester credit hours in professional course work.

    - 375 clock hours of supervised clinical observation/practice.

    - They also have completed a clinical fellowship, which consisted of at least 365 hours of full-time professional experience or its part-time equivalent. This fellowship must have been completed under the supervision of a speech/language pathologist who has a certificate of clinical competence.

■   They have passed a national examination administered by the Educational Testing Service .

3.   Are you licensed by the state?   Yes _____ No _____

Every state in the United States, except the District of Columbia, Idaho, Colorado, Michigan, and South Dakota, regulates the profession of speech/language pathology in some way. Go to www.asha.org/about/legislation-advocacy/state/associations to find out how your state regulates this profession. If applicable, the speech/language pathologist may be able to show you a copy of his or her license.

4.   How long have you been working as a speech/language pathologist? _____ years.

Of course, the number of years of experience that people have doesn't always correspond with their expertise. However, if you are interviewing a speech/language pathologist who is working in a private practice setting, ASHA recommends that he or she should have had at least three years prior experience working in a different setting before they began working in a private setting.

5.   Do you specialize in any particular area?
      Yes _____ No _____

_____ stuttering _____ voice _____ language _____ speech
_____ (other)

Speech/language pathologists are able to work with many different kinds of communication problems. During your first conversation about your child, it's important to give the speech/language pathologist as many details as you can about your concerns regarding your child's ability to communicate. It's important to find someone who specializes or has some expertise in the type of difficulty your child is experiencing.

6. What is the age of the majority of your patients?
    Adults: Ages ____
    Children: Ages: ____

You want to find a therapist who is used to working with children who are approximately the same age or close in age to your child. If you are conducting this interview in the therapist's office, be sure to observe what how the office is furnished. Are there puzzles or toys in the waiting room? Does the office seem cold and sterile, or is it inviting and kid friendly? If you call your local school district, ask to speak to the therapist who usually works with children in the same age range as your child. For example, if your child is four years old, ask, "May I speak to the speech/language therapist who works in your preschool program?"

7. Do you often attend workshops and seminars about _____ ? (Fill in information about the type of difficulties your child is having.)   Yes ____   No ____

It's important for professionals to keep informed about new therapy techniques and research. The well-educated therapist should be able to refer you to books, Web sites, or parent organizations to help you educate yourself about your child's difficulties.

SCHEDULING THE FIRST APPOINTMENT

Many times, the first thing a speech/language pathologist will want to do is to take a good look at your child's communication skills and discover if a communication problem exists, and the specific speech and language areas she may be having difficulty with. He or she will do this by evaluating or testing your child's skills. Note that an evaluation may also be called a diagnostic evaluation or an assessment. Moreover, an initial evaluation is important for measuring the progress your child makes in therapy. If your child is retested after a few months, the therapist can then compare the initial evaluation with the current up-to-date measure of progress.

When you are scheduling your first appointment, it may only be for a screening, rather than for a complete evaluation. Based on the information you'll have provided about your child's difficulties, the therapist will decide if a full evaluation or a screening is needed. A screening is a quick way to identify someone who is communicating within normal limits, as opposed to someone who may have a communication problem. Some therapists may choose to use informal methods, such as asking your child to count or to recite a familiar verse while they listen to how your child talks. Other therapists may prefer to use a standardized screening test. If you child fails a speech and language screening, usually the next step is a complete evaluation.

EXERCISE 22: Preparing for Your First Appointment

Directions: Please write the answers to the questions below in a journal or personal notebook that is reserved just for this use. This will give you more space to record the therapist's answers. Also, you'll be able to record any additional questions that come up during the interview, as well as the characteristic communication behaviors of your child at home. Bring this notebook to your first appointment.

Here are some questions to ask before your first appointment:

1. How soon can you see my child for an evaluation?
    _____ 1–2 weeks _____ 2–4 weeks _____ 4 or more weeks

    If the therapist is taking a three-week vacation and can't see you until two weeks after his or her return, this may not be advantageous to your child. Of course, you may have to wait a reasonable amount of time to get an appointment with someone who has a large practice.

2. What hours do you work? _____ morning _____ afternoon _____ after school _____ weekends

    It's important to schedule an appointment for a time when your child can be successful. For example, if you must schedule an appointment during her usual nap time or mealtime, this may not be advantageous.

3.   How long will the evaluation take?

_____ 1 hour _____ 2 hours _____ more than 2 hours

It's important to know whether the speech/language therapist will evaluate your child's skills in one session, or require the two of you to return several times to complete the evaluation. Also, you want to set aside enough time from your schedule so as not to feel rushed or hurried. If you are nervous about being late, this could cause your child to feel uneasy too.

4.   How should I prepare for the evaluation?

The younger your child, the more the evaluator may rely on you to relay information about her strengths and weaknesses. Ask what kinds of background history you'll need to provide so that you can answer the therapist's questions completely and accurately. Often, a blank case history form will be sent to you to fill out at home and bring to the first session. This information provides medical, social, and speech and language information for the speech/language pathologist to use as a starting point to understand your child's difficulties.

Perhaps you'll need to refresh your memory by looking in your child's "Baby Book" or by reminiscing with your spouse or child-care provider. Be ready to answer all health-related questions completely and accurately. Make a list of questions to ask the therapist to help you understand your child's difficulties, and ask what to expect in treatment. At home, watch your child and make a list for the therapist of characteristic communication behaviors that you observe your child doing.

5.   How should I prepare my child for the evaluation?

It's important to prepare your child and set the tone for the evaluation. Sometimes, when children are in an unfamiliar setting with a stranger who asks them to talk (not one of their favorite activities), the children won't demonstrate their true ability to communicate. Your child's level of comfort and cooperation will determine the success of the evaluation. Allow her to bring a special toy or book that may help "break the ice" between her and the therapist.

If you feel it would be helpful, explain in simple terms why you are going to see this special person and what is going to happen at his or her office. Encourage your child to ask you questions. Explain in simple terms, "You'll look at a lot of pictures. This special teacher will write down the words that you say, and will help you learn to say words. This person will show me how to help you, too, so I can understand when you say something important." On the day and time of your appointment, your child should be well rested, fed, and happy.

6. Once you have evaluated my child, how long must she wait for treatment if it is needed? _____ 1–2 weeks _____ 2–4 weeks _____ more than 4 weeks

Again, you must feel comfortable that the speech/language therapist has answered your question with a reasonable wait time.

IS SPEECH THERAPY EXPENSIVE?

As previously stated, a speech/language pathologist works in a variety of settings. Where you take your child for an evaluation and/or therapy will depend on your health insurance policy, your financial situation, the time you have, and the severity of your child's communication problems.

Free Services: Birth to Five Years Old

Usually, speech/language pathologists are members of the staff at your local school district. If your child (from birth to five years of age) meets your state's requirements, your local school district or county health department will be able to provide speech therapy free of charge. This is the result of two pieces of federal legislation described below.

The Education for All Handicapped Children Act (PL-94-142, enacted in 1975) mandates free and appropriate education for all children with handicaps from ages three to twenty-one. This includes an assessment to determine the nature and degree of a child's disability and the educational and resource services that are needed to ensure that child's success in learning.

In 1986, the federal government extended the legislation described above to include children from birth to three years of age. Children who are eligible include those who experience development delays in their communication skills and those who have been diagnosed with a physical or mental condition that has a high probability of resulting in developmental delay.

School-Age Children

If you have any questions or concerns about your child's communication skills, it is important to talk to her teacher or the speech/language pathologist as soon as possible. If your child meets the state requirements for eligibility for services, she may receive only speech therapy or she may receive these services as part of a more comprehensive educational plan during the regular school day.

Hospitals and University Clinics

Hospital and university clinics often base their fees for speech therapy services on your income. These services may be less expensive than a private practitioner. However, you may work with a student who is being supervised by an experienced speech/language pathologist.

Private Settings

In a private setting, fees for services are set by the provider and may be based on the type of service (evaluation, report, consultation, therapy) and how long the session lasts. Private speech/language pathologists are not mandated by state regulations that set up specific guidelines about who is eligible to receive therapy services. In some cases, your health insurance policy may pay for all or part of the cost of an evaluation and recommended treatment. Before your first visit, however, it would be wise to call your health insurance company to find out your policy specifications, whether you need a referral, and from whom.

EXERCISE 23: Preparation for Working in a Clinic, Hospital, or Private Setting

Here are some questions to ask the speech pathologist working in a clinical, hospital, or private setting:

1. How much do you charge for the evaluation?
    ____ No charge ____ Sliding scale based on your
    income ____ (amount)

2. How much do you charge for therapy sessions?
    ____ per ____ (fill in time)

3. Do you accept insurance payments?
    ____ Yes ____ No

4. Do you expect payment when services are rendered, or will you
    wait for the insurance company to send payment? ____ When
    services are rendered ____ Wait for insurance payment

5. If payment is expected, what kind of payments do you accept?
    ____ Cash ____ Credit cards ____ Personal check

6. Will you submit the necessary claim forms, or is that my responsi-
    bility? ____ Yes ____ My responsibility

7. Will I be charged if you are asked to submit additional insurance
    paperwork? ____ Yes ____ No

8. Will you help me appeal an unfavorable decision by my insurance
    company? ____ Yes ____ No

    (If you are denied, it is wise to ask for the denial in writing and
then ask what you need to do to appeal the denial.)

THE EVALUATION

In my experience, parents who take their child to a speech/language pathologist for an evaluation are often worried. They want to know why their child doesn't talk as well as her age peers, and how their child can be helped. For example, Mary Joy brought Joseph, four years and two months old, to the local hospital speech and hearing clinic. She was obviously worried and explained:

> People outside our family have a hard time understanding my son when he speaks. He uses the wrong sounds in words; for example, he calls a "car" a "tar" and pronounces his sister's name as "Tim" instead of "Kim." He calls himself "doe" instead of "Joe." When he is mad or really excited, he speaks too fast and all his words jumble together. He leaves out the /s/, too, not in all words, but in many. For example, he'll say, "hou" for "house" and "mou" for "mouse," and oh, he loves ba-ball. He says "ba-ball" for "baseball." When I ask him to repeat a word, he says it the same way he said it the first time. When we don't understand him, he says in a sad voice, "Never mind," and walks away.
>
> I feel so sorry for him and I just want to make it easier for him to talk. His preschool teacher told us that he doesn't talk very much in school and he likes to play by himself and doesn't really have many friends. He never raises his hand or talks with the other children. I think he is really getting frustrated and needs help.

The Process and Purpose of an Evaluation

Often the process and purpose of your child's initial speech evaluation will depend on the following factors:

- where you receive the services

- the type of difficulty your child has

- other physical, cognitive, or emotional problems that may coexist with your child's speech problem

- your child's age and attention span

- who does the evaluation

The Evaluation Parts

All testing materials and procedures must be selected and administered so as not to discriminate on the basis of race, culture, or gender. An evaluation has both a formal and an informal assessment.

Formal assessment. As part of the formal assessment, your child is given standardized tests. All children who take the test receive the same set of instructions and the same test items. These tests are scored the same for each child to ensure that the results are reliable. Many standardized tests sample a large range of skills and are *norm referenced*. This means that your child's score on the test will show how her performance compares to the average performance of a large sample of typically developing children who were also tested.

Next, a range is established that is considered the normal range for a child of a certain age. If your child's skills fall above this range, her skills are considered more developed than the average child of the same age; if her scores fall below the average range, she may need help.

Another type of standardized test is a *criterion-reference* test. These tests assess how well your child does on specific skills. When completed, this test usually provides a list of skills your child should work on, in the order that most typically developing children acquire these skills.

Informal assessment. Informal methods are used to help the therapist describe how your child uses language in her natural environment to communicate with others. Many different methods are used depending on the child's age and ability. The therapist may engage in free play with age-appropriate toys to encourage your child to speak naturally. For a younger child, the therapist may encourage the child to sing along to familiar songs or to follow a simple direction. Older children may be asked to read a passage or explain a picture, or they may be asked a direct question, such as "What's your favorite television show?" If it's possible, the therapist may observe how you and your child communicate. Just relax, and play and talk to her as you usually do. Learning how your child communicates in different natural settings may help the therapist give you suggestions about what you can do at home.

Other sources. If applicable, with your written permission, the therapist may contact your child's teacher and ask questions about how she communicates in the classroom and plays with other children, or how her academic skills are developing. Also, the speech/language pathologist may request evaluations by other professionals, such as an occupational therapist, physical therapist, or neurologist. This information will help the therapist to better understand your child and her needs.

Areas to Evaluate

The speech/language pathologist is interested in learning the communication skills your child has mastered, the skills she is currently learning, and those skills that warrant therapy. To do this, the therapist will want to take a close look at all the areas relevant to your child's communication skills. She may be assessed in some or all of the following areas:

1. **Hearing screening:** Often, the first step in an evaluation is a hearing test. Many speech/language pathologists can provide a hearing screening to identify potential hearing loss. If a child fails the screening, she should be referred to an audiologist for further evaluation.

2. **Developmental and recent case history:** Many times the speech/language pathologist will send you a written questionnaire, often in case history form, to gather information about your child before the evaluation. This may give the pathologist some idea of the kinds of difficulties your child has and what would be the best way to do the assessment. Others may ask you questions when you arrive at the office for your first appointment. These questions may include information about your child's:

    ■   **Physical motor development:** This refers to the way a child's muscles work and how her body has developed. *Sample questions:* "Does your child seem clumsy, or does she fall down a lot?"

- **Cognitive development:** This refers to the way a child's brain makes sense out of what she hears, sees, tastes, smells, or touches.
  Sample question: "Can your child understand a simple direction?"

- **Social/emotional development:** This refers to the way a child manages emotions and relates to other people in her environment.
  Sample question: "Does your child recognize familiar people?"

- **Speech/language development:** This refers to the way a child learns to understand others and to express her own thoughts and ideas.
  Sample question: "How does your child express her wants and needs?"

3. **Articulation testing:** The therapist will administer formal and informal tests to asses your child's production of each phoneme in English in the initial, medial, and final positions of words. In many formal tests of articulation, a child is asked to name a picture and the therapist records if the specified sound and its position in the word was said correctly.

4. **Phonological process testing:** If your child exhibits a lot of speech errors, the therapist will do a phonological process analysis. He or she will analyze your child's errors and determine the sound simplification strategies she is using (phonological processes). This may be done as part of direct testing, using objects or pictures, or as part of a conversational speech sample.

5. **Oral peripheral examination:** An oral peripheral examination is an assessment of the structure and function of the muscles in and around the face. This is done in order to determine if there are physical factors influencing your child's pronunciation of sounds. As part of the oral peripheral examination, the therapist may observe your child's facial structure at rest and in motion. This will help him or her to determine if your child is experiencing any weakness, paralysis, or poor coordination of the speech

musculature; difficulties in planning motor behavior; and/or difficulties with sequencing sounds. This type of observation at rest
includes these factors: studying the appearance of the lips, the
size of the tongue, and how this compares to the size of the
mouth. When observing your child's oral mechanisms in motion,
your child may be asked to lift her tongue to try to touch her
nose, or lower her tongue to try to touch her chin.

6. **Receptive language testing:** The therapist may use formal and
informal testing to see how much language your child can understand. During formal testing, your child may be asked to point to
pictures of the words that the therapist says. During an informal
assessment, she may be asked to follow age-appropriate
commands.

7. **Expressive language:** The therapist may use both formal and
informal testing to examine all the ways your child can communicate. During formal testing, she may be asked to name pictures or
objects. During informal testing, the therapist wants to get a sample of how your child talks spontaneously in her natural environment. He or she may take a close look at this language sample to
determine the following:

- What is the average number of words your child uses to
  express herself?

- Does she speak in complete, grammatically correct sentences, and can she ask and answer questions appropriately for her developmental age level?

- Is her conversational speech easy or hard to understand?
  Is her conversational speech easier or harder to understand than the single-word productions she made during
  the testing?

- What does she do to get her message across? Does she
  use a lot of gestures or pantomime? Is she aware of the
  needs of the listener, and can she take turns in a conversation and remain on topic?

- Does she speak too slow or too fast?

- Does she hesitate or repeat sounds or syllables often?

8. **Voice and resonance:** Through informal testing, the examiner will determine if your child's voice quality and resonance are appropriate. *Voice quality* refers to how the voice sounds. For example, someone's voice can be too harsh, too soft, or too hoarse and, in turn, those qualities can interfere with the message the child is trying to say. *Resonance* refers to the tonal quality of a child's voice. For example, when sounds are always resonated in the nasal cavity instead of the mouth, that person would sound as if he or she always had a cold.

9. **Feeding and swallowing evaluation:** If a child has severe communication problems, the therapist may want to formally and informally assess feeding and swallowing.

10. **Intelligibility ratings:** The therapist may use formal or informal measures to judge how well your child's speech is understood by an unfamiliar listener.

11. **Stimulability testing:** The therapist may use formal or informal tests to assess your child's ability to imitate a sound when given visual, auditory, or tactile prompts, even though she doesn't say this particular sound correctly in her spontaneous speech. This measure is used to help the therapist determine which sounds might be easiest to correct in therapy.

Getting the Results

After the evaluation, the speech/language pathologist should make arrangements to discuss the results with you in a timely fashion. In most cases, you will be given a written report. The report may include the following:

- **Child's identifying information:** Name, date of birth, age, address, phone number, parent's name(s), school status, date of the evaluation.

- **Reason for referral:** A statement summarizing why the child needed an evaluation.

- **Background information:** A summary of the information you provided for the case history form or information from other professionals, such as your child's pediatrician or teacher.

- **Test results and discussion:** Results of all the formal and informal testing that the speech/language pathologist performed and an explanation of what these results mean.

- **Summary:** This section usually reviews all the testing results in a concise manner and includes a diagnosis.

- **Recommendations:** This section outlines the therapist's recommendations. If therapy is recommended, the recommendations may include information about how many sessions per week and how long each session should be. The therapist may also recommend additional testing by other professionals.

EXERCISE 24: Questions to Ask about the Evaluation

You should feel comfortable asking the speech/language pathologist questions about the results of the evaluation. If you do not agree with the testing results, discuss your disagreements with the therapist. Explain why you feel these tests are a good estimate of your child's skills or why they underestimate how well she communicates at home. This exercise is only a sample of the many questions you may want to ask. Write down any additional questions you may have in your journal and be sure to bring those questions to your meeting with the speech/language pathologist.

1. What areas of communication did you test?

2. What are my child's specific communication strengths and weaknesses?

3. What do these results mean? Many times a speech/language pathologist reports the results of a standardized test in terms of

developmental age score, developmental quotient, percentile ranking, or standard score. You may not understand these terms, so be sure to ask as many questions as necessary to be sure you understand what the reported score means for the particular tests that were given.

4. Why are you recommending _____ (the specific recommendations in your child's report)? Make sure you fully understand all of the therapist's recommendations. If your child is found to be ineligible for speech therapy, discuss the reasons surrounding this decision. Ask for recommendations on how to help your child at home and find out when the therapist recommends your child's skills should be rescreened or retested. If you feel it is necessary, seek a second opinion.

5. How will you use these results to plan therapy goals?

6. Can you give me some suggestions on how to help my child at home that I can begin right away?

7. Would you suggest that I have my child evaluated by any other professionals at this time?

8. How often will you discuss my child's therapy progress with me?

9. Can you give me any indication as to how long my child may need therapy?

What to Expect in Therapy

What happens during speech therapy will depend on the type and severity of your child's difficulties, her age, her ability to pay attention, and where the therapy takes place. For example, a child with an articulation problem may work on one or more sounds. In therapy, she may learn to hear the difference between the correct and incorrect production of the error sounds that the therapist says. Next, she may learn to produce these sounds in isolation, syllables, words, and sentences. Finally, she will learn to carry over the correct production of her error sounds into her spontaneous speech outside the therapy setting. If your child has therapy to reduce her use of phono-logical processes, the therapist may develop her awareness and use of sounds. Most importantly, speech therapy should be conducted in an accepting and entertaining atmosphere. Each session should be enjoyable as well as therapeutic.

KEEP COMMUNICATION LINES OPEN

It's important that you play an active role in your child's therapy program. Make a plan for keeping in touch with the therapist. If you are taking your child to a hospital, clinic, or private office, the thera-pist may be able to talk to you briefly at the end of each therapy ses-sion. Ask the therapist to write down specific instructions for you to practice at home with your child, or tips on how to stimulate sounds as you go about your daily life activities. This will not only help and reinforce what your child learns in speech therapy, it will also help her to transfer the skills she learns in the structured speech class environment to a more natural home environment. Find out if you can observe the therapist working with your child, either through a two-way mirror or by sitting in the therapy room during the session.

If your child receives speech therapy as part of her natural school day, she may receive a "speech book" that comes with home-work activities to practice with you at home. These activities will vary depending on the goals and the specific skills your child is working on in therapy. In the first stages, the homework assignment might be to draw or cut out pictures from a magazine that illustrate your child's target sound.

As she progresses and can hear the difference between the correct and incorrect production of her target sound and can make this sound correctly in words, the homework assignment might be for you to listen and reinforce the correct productions of sounds the same way you would practice for a spelling test. Ask the therapist to write comments in the book, and you do the same. Note that it's important to inform the therapist if something in your child's life changes dramatically that might affect her speech, for example, the birth of new sibling, a family member or relative becoming ill, or a medical condition.

A FINAL WORD

Throughout this book, I have stressed how important it is to seek professional help if you have any questions or concerns about your child's development. In this chapter, I've outlined who can help, how to find help, where to find help, and what to expect during the evaluation and therapy. Having this information may help you to ask questions, feel more confident, and, most importantly, prod you to make an appointment for your child's communication skills to be evaluated sooner rather than later. Good luck and remember, have fun while helping your child to speak more clearly.

Glossary

Age of acquisition: This term refers to the age at which 75 percent (sometimes 90 percent) of children in research studies are able to say a particular sound correctly in the initial, medial, and final positions of words (Templin 1957).

American Speech-Language-Hearing Association (ASHA): This organization is the professional, scientific, and credentialing association for audiologists, speech/language pathologists, and speech, language, and hearing scientists.

Apraxia: This is a disorder of the nervous system that affects a child's ability to plan the motor movements needed to produce sounds.

Articulation: This means the ability to produce the speech sounds that make up syllables, words, and sentences.

Articulators: In order to make sounds, we must control and move our articulators. Articulators include our lips, teeth, tongue, jaw, and various areas in the roof of the mouth.

Audiologists: These are professionals who identify and assess disorders of the hearing and balance system of children and adults. They select, fit, and dispense amplification systems, such as hearing aids and related devices. They also program cochlear implants, and provide instruction, rehabilitation, and counseling services to enhance human communication. A graduate degree (doctorate or master) is required to practice.

Babbling: This is vocal play or the sounds babies make when they combine a consonant and vowel and then repeat the same syllable over and over again; for example, "baba."

Blend: A word with a blend contains two consonants linked together. For example, "sl" in the word "slide" is a blend.

Communication: This means the exchange of thoughts or messages using speech, symbols, or writing.

Conductive hearing loss: This is a type of hearing loss resulting from a problem with a part of the outer or middle ear.

Evaluation: This means to use formal and informal assessments to take a comprehensive look at your child's communication skills, and to discover the specific speech and language areas with which your child may have difficulties.

Expressive language: This is the language used to express thoughts and feelings, answer questions, and relate events. It includes words, tone of voice, gestures, and rate of speech.

Fluency: This means the flow or rhythm of a person's speech. Problems with fluency are often referred to as "stuttering."

Functional articulation problem: This refers to an inability to produce all of the standard sounds of a language. There is, however, no known cause for these difficulties.

Hearing loss: When there is a problem with one or more parts of a child's ear or ears that prevents the child from hearing sounds properly, that is called a hearing loss.

Intelligibility: This refers to how well your child's speech is understood or comprehended by others.

Jargon: For speech pathologists, this term is used to mean the early true language sounds that children make when they put vowels and consonants together and use real tone and inflection. For example, when a baby says, "bagada," that's called jargon.

Language: This refers to a set of symbols used by people to communicate. These symbols can be written, spoken, or even gestures, as in sign languages.

Language disorder: This refers to a noticeable problem with understanding and/or expressing thoughts and ideas.

Morphology: This refers to the individual elements of a language, such as root words, prefixes, and suffixes. When a child understands the morphological rules of his language, he can understand and speak words he has never heard or spoken previously.

Oral motor: This means the physical makeup of a person's mouth.

Organic problems: When the cause of an articulation problem is organic, it is the result of structural or brain problems.

Otitis media: This is the medical term for an ear infection.

Phonation: This refers to what takes place in our larynx and vocal cords (also called vocal folds) that enables us to produce audible sounds.

Phoneme: This is the smallest unit of speech that corresponds to the letters of an alphabetic writing system.

Phonological awareness: This is the ability to notice, manipulate, and think about the sounds in language.

Phonological processes: This refers to mastering the sound patterns of a language. A phonological process is a strategy used by children between one and one-half years to four years of age to simplify their production of adult speech sounds.

Phonology: This refers to the sound system of a language and the rules that govern how the sounds are combined to convey meaning.

Pragmatics: These are the rules that govern how we use our language in social situations.

Screening: This refers to a quick way to identify someone who is communicating within normal limits as opposed to someone who may have a communication problem.

Semantics: This refers to the meaning of words and the ability to understand and express words to convey meaning.

Sensory hearing loss: This refers to a type of hearing loss that occurs when there is a problem in the inner ear or in the nerves that send the sounds to the brain.

Speech: This refers to the sounds that are made when a message is communicated verbally.

Speech/language pathologist: This is the title of the professional who has been trained to evaluate and treat children and adults suffering from a variety of communication problems. This individual may also be referred to as a "speech/language therapist" or a "speech/language specialist."

Syntax: This refers to the grammar or the rules that govern sentence construction, including word order and how to ask questions.

Tongue thrust: When people do not develop normal swallowing patterns, they may protrude their tongue between their teeth while speaking or swallowing, and when the tongue is at rest.

Unintelligible: This refers to speech that cannot be understood.

Voice: This means the sound that is produced by the larynx. The pitch, loudness, and quality of a person's voice should be appropriate for the individual.

References

American Academy of Otolaryngology-Head and Neck Surgery. 2003. *Doctor, Is My Baby's Hearing Normal? Determine If Your Child Has a Hearing Loss.* Alexandria, Va.: American Academy of Otolaryngology-Head and Neck Surgery.

American Speech-Language-Hearing Association (ASHA). 2000. *Communication Facts. Science and Research Department.* Rockville, Md.: American Speech-Language-Hearing Association.

Arndt, J., and C. Healey. 2001. Concomitant disorders in school-age children who stutter. *Language, Speech, and Hearing Services in School* 32:68-78.

Bowey, J. A., and J. Francis. 1991. Phonological analysis as a function of age and exposure to reading instruction. *Applied Psycholinguistics* 12:91-121.

Bryant, P. E. 1990. Phonological development and reading. In *Children's Difficulties in Reading, Spelling, and Writing: Challenges and Responses*, edited by P. D. Pumfrey and C. D. Elliot. London: The Falmer Press.

Bryant, P. E., M. MacLean, L. L. Bradley, and J. Crossland. 1990. Rhyme and alliteration, phoneme detection, and learning to read. *Developmental Psychology* 26:429-438.

Casteel, R., S. Fletcher, and D. Bradley. 1961. Tongue-thrust swallow, speech articulation, and age. *Journal of Speech and Hearing Disorders* 26:201-208.

Christensen, C. A. 1997. Onset, rhymes and phonemes in learning to read. *Scientific Studies of Reading* 4:341-358.

Cunningham, M., and E. Cox. 2003. Hearing assessment in infants and children: Recommendations beyond neonatal screening. *Pediatrics* 111(2):436-440.

Davis, E. 1937. The development of linguistic skills in twins, singletons with siblings, and only children from age five to ten years. Minneapolis: University of Minnesota Press.

Ediger, M. 1999. Reading and vocabulary development. *Journal of Instructional Psychology* 26(1):7-15.

Ehri, L. C., S. R. Nunes, D. M. Willows, B. V. Schuster, Z. Yaghoub-Zadeh, and T. Shanahan. 2001. Phonemic awareness instruction helps children learn to read: Evidence from the National Reading Panel's Meta-Analysis. *Reading Research Quarterly* 36:250-287.

Fox, A. V., B. Dodd, and V. Howard. 2002. Risk factors for speech disorders in children. *International Journal of Language and Communication Disorders* 37(2):117-131.

Friel-Patti, S. 1998. Implications of auditory processing on emergent literacy. *American Speech-Language-Hearing Association Division 1 Newsletter: Language Learning and Education* (May):25-26.

Gravel J., and I. Wallace. 1995. Early otitis media, auditory abilities and educational risk. *American Journal of Speech-Language Pathology* 3:89-94.

————. 1998. Language, speech, and educational outcomes of otitis media. *The Journal of Otolaryngology* 27:17-25.

Gregory, H., and D. Hill. 1993. Differential evaluation and differential therapy for stuttering children. In *Stuttering and Related Disorders of Fluency*, edited by R. Curlee. New York: Thieme-Stratton.

Hodson, B. W. 1998. Research and practice: Applied phonology. *Topics in Language Disorders* 18:58-70.

Hodson, B. W., and E. P. Paden. 1981. Phonological processes which characterize unintelligible and intelligible speech in early childhood. *Journal of Speech and Hearing Disorders* 46:369-373.

Hughes, F. P., L. D. Noppe, and I. C. Noppe. 1996. *Child Development.* Upper Saddle River, New Jersey: Prentice Hall.

Huttenlocher, J., M. Vasilyeva, E. Cymerman, and S. Levine. 2002. Language input and child syntax. *Cognitive Psychology* 45: 337-374.

Kent, R. D. 2000. A longitudinal case study of ALS: Effects of listener familiarity and proficiency on intelligibility judgments. *American Journal of Speech-Language Pathology* 3:230-240.

King, P. 2002. Talking it out: The word on stuttering. *Parents Express* (September):16.

Koralek, D. 1997. *Ready, Set, Read: Early Activity Guides for Families and Caregivers. A Project of The Corporation for National Services, United States Department of Education, and the United States Department of Health and Human Services.* Washington, D.C.: Government Printing Office.

Kuhl, P. K., K. A. Williams, F. Lacerda, K. N. Stevens, and B. Lindblom. 1992. Linguistic experience alters phonetic perception in infants by 6 months of age. *Science* 255:606-608.

Liberman, I. Y., D. Shankweiler, and A. M. Liberman. 1989. The alphabetic principle and learning to read. In *Phonology and Reading Disability: Solving the Reading Puzzle,* edited by D. Shankweiler and I. Y. Liberman, 1–33. Ann Arbor, Mich.: University of Michigan Press.

McDonald, E. 1964. *Articulation Testing and Treatment: A Sensory-Motor Approach.* Pittsburgh, Penn.: Stanwick House.

Menyuk, P., M. Chesnick, J. W. Liebergott, B. Korngold, R. D. Agostino, and A. Belanger. 1991. Predicting reading problems in at-risk children. *Journal of Speech and Hearing Research* 34: 893-904.

Nathan, L., J. Stackhouse, N. Goulandris, and M. J. Snowling. 2004. The development of early literacy skills among children with speech difficulties: A test of the "critical age hypothesis." *Journal of Speech, Language and Hearing Research* 47:377-391.

National Association of School Psychologists (NASP). 2002. Creating successful readers by developing phonological awareness skills: Suggestions for parents and teachers. NASP Communique 29 (4):1-7.

National Center on Birth Defects and Developmental Disabilities. 2003. *The Genetics of Hearing Loss.* Washington, D.C.: Centers for Disease Control and Prevention.

National Institute on Deafness and Other Communication Disorders. 1997. *NIDCD Fact Sheet: Stuttering.* Washington D.C.: Government Printing Office.

————s. 1995. *Research in Human Communication.* Bethesda, Md.: NIH Publication No. 92-3317.

Perkins, W. 1977. *Speech Pathology: An Applied Behavioral Science.* St. Louis, Mo.: Mosby.

Peterson-Falzone, S., M. Hardin-Jones, M. Karnell, and B. J. McWilliams. 2001. *Cleft Palate Speech.* St. Louis, Mo.: C. V. Mosby.

Quigley, S. P., and R. E. Kretschmer. 1982. *The Education of Deaf Children.* Baltimore: University Park Press.

Roth, F. P., and B. Baden. 2001. Investing in emergent literacy intervention: A key role for speech-language pathologists. *Seminars in Speech and Language* 22(3):163-173.

Schaefer, E., and T. DiGeronimo. 2000. *Ages and Stages.* New York: John Wiley & Sons, Inc.

Shore, R. Families and Work Institute. 1996. Rethinking the Brain: New Insights into Early Development. New York: Families and Work Institute.

Smit, A. B., L. Hand, J. Freilinger, J. B. Bernthal, and A. Bird. 1990. The Iowa Articulation Norms Project and its Nebraska replication. *Journal of Speech and Hearing Disorders* 55:779-798.

Stackhouse, J. 1997. Phonological awareness: Connecting speech and literacy problems, In *Perspectives in Applied Phonology,* edited by

B. Hodson and M. Edwards, 157-196. Gaithersburg, Md.: Aspen Publishers, Inc.

Stanovich, K. 1996. Does reading make you smarter? Literacy and the development of verbal intelligence. In *Advances in Child Development and Behavior*, edited by H. Reese, 133-180. San Diego, Calif.: Academic Press.

Task Force on Newborn and Infant Hearing. 1999. Newborn and infant hearing loss: detection and intervention. *Pediatrics* 103 (2):527-530.

Templin, M. 1957. *Certain Language Skills in Children*. Minneapolis, MN: University of Minnesota Press.

Torgesen, J. K., R. K. Wagner, and C. A. Rashotte. 1997. The prevention and remediation of severe reading disabilities: Keeping the end in mind. *Scientific Studies of Reading* 1:217-234.

Winitz, H. 1969. *Articulatory Acquisition and Behavior*. New York: Appleton-Century-Crofts.

Yairi, E., and N. Ambrose. 1992. A longitudinal study of stuttering in children: A preliminary report. *Journal of Speech and Hearing Research* 25:755-768.

Zielhuis, G., G. Rach, and P. van den Broek. 1989. Screening for otitis media with effusion in preschool children. *The Lancet* 11: 311-313.

Bibliography of Children's Books

The Accidental Zucchini: An Unexpected Alphabet by Max Grover (1997). Greensboro, N.C.: Voyager Books.

Animalia by Graeme Base (1997). New York: Harry N. Abrams.

Berenstain's B Book by Stan and Jan Berenstain (1997). New York: Random House Books for Young Readers.

Berlioz the Bear by Jan Brett (1996). New York: Putnam Publishing Group.

Bob's Busy Saw by Kiki Thorpe (2002). New York: Simon Spotlight.

A Bug, a Bear, and a Boy Go to School by David McPhail (1999). Minneapolis, Minn.: Sagebrush Bound.

Carl Goes Shopping by Alexandra Day (1992). New York: Farrar, Straus and Giroux.

The Cat in the Hat Comes Back by Dr. Seuss (1958). New York: Random House Books for Young Readers.

Charlie and the Chocolate Factory by Roald Dahl (2002). New York: Knopf Books for Young Readers.

Chicka Chicka Boom Boom by Bill Martin and John Archambault (2000). New York: Aladdin Picture Books.

Cows in the Kitchen by June Crebbin (2003). Cambridge, Mass.: Candlewick Press.

Don't Forget the Bacon by Pat Hutchings (1989). New York: Harper Trophy.

Don't Get Lost by Pat Hutchins (2004). New York: Greenwillow Books.

Each Peach Pear Plum by Janet and Allan Ahlberg (1999). New York: Viking Books.

Fire Truck by Peter Sis (1998). New York: Harper Festival.

Fix-It by David McPhail (1987). Des Moines, Iowa: Perfection Learning Corporation.

The Foot Book by Dr. Suess (1996). New York: Random House Children's Books.

A Girl, a Goat, and a Goose by David McPhail (2000). Minneapolis, Minn.: Sagebrush Bound.

Giraffes Can't Dance by Giles Andreae and Guy Parker-Rees (1999). New York: Scholastic Books.

Goodnight Moon by Margaret Wise Brown (1991). New York: Harper Festival.

Goosie by Olivier Dunrea (2002). Boston: Houghton Mifflin.

The Happy Lion by Louise Fatio (2004). New York: Knopf Books for Young Readers.

Hop on Pop by Dr. Seuss (1991). New York: Random House.

How Many Kisses Do You Want Tonight? by Varsha Bajaj (2004). New York: Little, Brown and Co.

If You Give a Moose a Muffin by Laura Joffe Numeroff (1995). New York: Harper Collins Children's Books.

Jack and the Beanstalk by Steven Kellogg (1997). New York: Harper Trophy.

The Kissing Hand by Audrey Penn (1993). Lanham, Md.: National Book Network Press.

Larabee by Kevin Luthardt (2004). Atlanta, Ga.: Peachtree.

The Little Blue Rabbit by Angela McAllister (2003). London: Bloomsbury Publishing.

Little Rabbit Goes to School by Harry Horse (2004). Atlanta, Ga.: Peachtree.

Lizard Walinsky by Robert Baker (2004). New York: Little, Brown and Co.

The Mitten: A Ukrainian Folktale by Jan Brett (1996). New York: Putnam Publishing Group.

More, More, More, Said the Baby by Vera Williams (1997). New York: Greenwillow.

One Odd Old Owl by Paul Adshead (1996). Wiltshire, U.K.: Child's Play International Ltd.

Pat the Bunny by Dorothy Kunhardt (2000). New York: Golden Books.

Peter's Chair by Ezra Jack Keats (1998). New York: Puffin Books.

Phonemic Awareness Songs & Rhymes (Grades Pre-K to 2) by Wiley Blevins (2004). New York: Scholastic Prof. Books Division.

Playing with Sound to Strengthen Beginning Reading Skills by Jo Fitzpatrick (1997). Huntington Beach, Calif.: Creative Teaching Press.

The Read-Aloud Handbook by Jim Trelease (2001). New York: Penguin USA.

Read-Aloud Rhymes for the Very Young by Jack Prelutsky (1986). New York: Knopf Books for Young Readers.

Roller Coaster by Marla Frazee (2003). New York: Harcourt Children's Books.

See the Fly Fly by Catherine Chase (1979). Tempe, Ariz.: Dandelion Press.

Sheep in a Jeep by Nancy E. Shaw (1997). Boston, Mass.: Houghton Mifflin.

The Snowy Day by Ezra Jack Keats (1962). New York: Viking Books.

Ten Little Ladybugs by Melanie Gerth (2000). Los Angeles: Piggy Toes Press.

Where Is Everybody? An Unexpected Alphabet by Eve Merriam (1992). Upper Saddle River, N.J.: Pearson Prentice Hall.

Where's Spot by Eric Hill (2003). New York: Puffin Books.

Zella, Zack and Zodiac by Bill Peet (1989). Boston: Houghton Mifflin.

A Zoo for Mister Muster by Arnold Lobel (1962). New York: Harper Collins.